Daily Journaling for Self-Injury Recovery:
A Therapists' Guide for Clients

AuthorHouse™
1663 Liberty Drive
Bloomington, IN 47403
www.authorhouse.com
Phone: 1-800-839-8640

First published by AuthorHouse 10/15/09

ISBN: 978-1-4490-4005-5 (e)
ISBN: 978-1-4490-3908-0 (sc)

Library of Congress Control Number: 2009910962

Printed in the United States of America
Bloomington, Indiana

This book is printed on acid-free paper.

Daily Journaling for Self-Injury Recovery:
A Therapists' Guide for Clients

K. R. Juzwin, Psy.D.

This journal is a set of exercises to be used by therapists to help people who are struggling with self-destructive behaviors and thinking and want to change. This is a long process, one that many people don't understand. Self-injury and self-destructive behaviors and thinking can become such a big part of life and relationships, that the thought of change is overwhelming. It developed out of requests from therapists for something tangible to give clients. It isn't perfectly polished, is a bit more theory than conversation in parts, but it is a start.

I have had the privilege of learning from many people struggling with chronic and acute self-destructive behavior. They taught me their perspective, how this behavior is helpful to them. They are more courageous than they know. I have also had the privilege of learning from and working with many skilled and talented clinicians. One significant influence in my thinking is John Levitt, Ph.D. My efforts at condensing some of his teachings here are out of respect to his conceptualization and translation of ideas into practice. I encourage clinicians to read his theoretical model further. I am a better clinician and have stronger conceptualization skills because of his generous mentoring and teaching. Having a sound philosophy and set of practices parallels what we ask our patients to do in creating a purposeful and mindful life. He taught me to endeavor to be a guide to the client, who is the expert of their own life.

I also continue to learn from the many skilled clinicians from Alexian Brothers Medical Center and Behavioral Health Hospital, where I now practice. I also thank my colleagues at Alexian Brothers Self-Injury Recovery Services at who have encouraged me in my consultation, teaching and supervisory work, above and beyond my clinical work. I thank them for finding my contributions helpful to them, and for sharing their feedback. My other teachers include clinicians at the hospital and my colleagues in my outpatient practices, who shared some very difficult clinical experiences and cases. Many of us were fortunate to train with Dr. Levitt, and the time was rich with learning and development. I especially thank this group of clinicians who helped shaped my skills and philosophical outlook. I know I have left people out, for that I'm sorry. Annmarie Belmonte and Kathy Zachary, thank you for your encouragement in this project, and the time, effort and generous feedback about this work.

I also thank my colleagues at Alexian Brothers Behavioral Health Hospital, where our units and practice are, who have encouraged and supported me in my consultation, teaching and supervisory work and clinical work. The supervision and consultation I've received from my colleagues and supervisors has helped me be an eager student as I continue to develop. I especially thank Cliff Saper, Ph.D. and Francine McGouey, C.E.O, who set a standard I hope I can continue to emulate. And, my gratitude to those who kept on me about finishing this project! On a personal level to the foundation and framework for my life: my family and extended family/friends for their belief in my efforts.

I have made diligent effort to appropriately site the quotes I used. I took them from the public domain, in very auspicious places such as fortune cookies, quotes from the newspaper, church programs, bill boards, off of pens, sticky pads, thoughts of the day, and the emails quotes and statements of friends. Some of them are mantras I've heard people use. If I have misquoted, or misattributed quotes, I sincerely apologize. I think having mantras can be very important and give us something to anchor ourselves in times when we are overwhelmed. Many are mantras I've heard and used throughout my career and have found helpful. These simple words of wisdom can serve as guides and reminders of what we are moving towards, and create mindfulness and awareness.

I hope you find this helpful in your healing and growth process.

krj

This is dedicated to:

Those who are taking the leap of faith, believing in themselves.
Those who are willing to be courageous.
Those who are willing to be more than they are in this moment.
Those who see the past as part of where they have been, but not necessarily of where they have to go.
Those who are willing to take a risk into a future they are creating.
Those who are willing to accept they have value because they exist.
Those who Guide, and to those who let us come along with them.
Those who work to practice what they teach!

Daily Journaling for Self-Injury Recovery:
A Therapists' Guide for Clients
A Note of Introduction & Requests

A note to people with self-injury: If you are struggling with self-injury or other kinds of self-destructive thoughts and behaviors, talk to your therapist *before* you begin any work in this book. And, please work with a therapist while working on this journal. It is not recommended that you work without extra support and guidance of a therapist. This can provide you guidance and keep you from becoming further overwhelmed or struggle with managing. If you are working with a therapist or counselor, follow their recommendations and their lead. Each page has a specific lesson or message. The goal is to work slowly, learning each lesson, and connecting your mind and body in the lesson and being in the present. The goal is to create safety and connection needed to develop healthy self-management. Your therapist will help you learn how to not be overwhelmed and to keep you safe.

With the guidance of your therapist, work one page at a time, and you can redo them over and over. You can use words, colors, symbols, pictures to help express yourself. But, please do it mindfully and with an eye to your future. It is important to understand that recovery includes connecting with, and being aware of, both your mind and body, and accepting the connection that exists between them. Acknowledging the connection between mind and body and biology/physiology is very important in developing self-regulation. Understanding the experiential mind & body work is so important in learning to live within one's own body.

It helps if you bring these in to talk with your therapist, and talk honestly about your work. You'll notice the use of boxes to work in. This is purposeful, they help contain and keep you structured and focused. Unless you are able to keep yourself safe, and manage your destructive feelings and impulses, freer and unstructured journaling can become dangerous, provocative and triggering. So if you are new in this process, the more focus and structure, the better. You can rework the assignments as many times as you need them.

A note to Therapists & Counselors: Why do written work and talk about it therapy? Journaling is a part of the therapy process. And, when used to augment therapy, it can be a powerful and helpful tool. It is important to have focus on what you want to achieve when you are helping someone towards change and something that feels impossible and brand new. This journal is to give therapists working with people with deliberate self-destructive impulses, urges and behaviors a structured way to work on one important lesson at a time.

In my experience working with people who self-injure, I have learned from their struggles with self-regulation, destructive impulses and what they find helpful. A number of these journaling assignments were developed while working with people in recovery who are learning to think in differently way about a difficult set of problems, impacting their lives greatly. I tried to include these lessons in this book.

One lesson I want to emphasize is the *language* in this journal. It is deliberate. I get feedback that sometimes that the language is somewhat formal and the constructs are complicated. This is probably true. I think my patients are a pretty intelligent group of people, and I adjust my language to help the individual master the constructs. It is, in my opinion, my job to work through and teach the patient the language. It gives them the language to speak their minds. *It is our job as clinicians to not just photocopy written exercises and tell our patients to do them.* When we discuss the materials on these pages, we are teaching them:

- Language skills for communication and expression.
- How to interact, get their needs met appropriately.
- How to tolerate frustration.
- How to tolerate having to ask for help appropriately.
- How to tolerate getting helped.
- How to tolerate interaction and closeness.
- How to ask questions and think about things, and then sit with them.
- It is an opportunity to have healthy mentoring interactions which help with attachment, modeling and social skills.
- It is an opportunity to build off of their existing skills, intelligence and resources.
- It is a teaching opportunity for expression, thinking and understanding!

There are many components needing to be addressed in treatment. These include creating a working agreement, healthy limits and boundaries, structure and accountability. Much of what we clinicians do, to a great degree, is healthy parenting and helping to develop healthy attachments, age-appropriate skills development and maturity. Expecting that someone can self-manage is an important belief, and it is reasonable to believe this growth is going to be difficult. Many of our patients don't understand that their feelings are *reasonable*, and serve as data that something important is going on. Feelings aren't facts though, and it is important *to think reasonably* through our problems. It is our job to help them learn these lessons.

This work is based on the theoretical concepts of self-management and learning to tolerate and manage reactions to feelings. There are many influences to this approach to self-regulation, most specifically of structural process model developed by John Levitt, Ph.D. (2004); other influences come from cognitive behavior, family systems, object relations, mind/body approaches and developmental theories.

This work is not designed to emphasize memory-based recovery work. The focus in these activities is learning to manage the effects of the past in the present here and now. It involves being alive and grounded in the present and creating a new future, using the past as a frame of reference only. In our philosophy, the focus on traumatic memory work when someone can't manage the day to day life may be overwhelming, and cause trauma in the present. *There is a time and a place for that work: after safety, security and physical well-being are established.*

- *Know what your goal is, every day, every minute.* What do you want? You can't get a new way to what you want with old thoughts, feelings and behaviors that haven't worked.
- *Be willing to try something new and different.* The goal is to think differently about something you've done that hasn't worked in the way you've wanted.
- *Turn your thoughts into actions.* Practice what you write. So be mindful about what you are writing.
- *Tolerate your feelings. Think your way through*…Pay attention to your reactions when you are working. Make sure you can manage your thoughts, feelings and reactions safely. Meaning, not dissociating or hurting yourself.
- *Practice, practice and then practice more. Create opportunities to* think differently.
- *Tolerate your feelings. They can't hurt you; practice your deep breathing and focus.* Practice tolerating feelings, behaving differently and thinking about getting what you really want.
- *Practice tolerating feeling, and tolerate it. Feelings have a beginning, middle and an end. Sometimes the middle really stinks and feels like there is no end. Feelings aren't dangerous or harmful. The behaviors you use might be though. Your feelings may be uncomfortable but they aren't dangerous.*
- *Manage your breathing stay focused and grounded in the present.* If you find yourself getting overwhelmed, go back and work on creating safety (Core Exercise A, Getting Grounded). Remember to work mind and body connected! Recognize when you get overwhelmed, and if that happens, practice grounding yourself using Core Exercise A & B.
- *Remember you create your goal, and have endless opportunities to practice creating something new.* The goal is to be healthy, create choices for yourself, and be mindful about your life.
- *Stay grounded and connected to your present moment.*
- *Give yourself permission to try something new.*
- *Your behaviors are better indictors of your investment and motivation than your words.*
- *If you wait to "feel better" before you try something new, you'll always get what you've always got!!*
- You are not your problem behaviors!
- THINK your way through your feelings, using your goals and values as your guide. You are responsible for your actions.
- Use your *words*, not your behaviors to express yourself.
- You can stop at any time, and ground yourself, calm down and refocus.

Helpful hint:
- Make a deck of note cards with a helpful statement on each one. The statements can be something you find helpful, with a short sentence on each to cue you about how to THINK your way through your life, changing from reacting or feeling.
- While reading your cards, practice your breathing and relaxing.
- Picture yourself accepting the words.
- Practice living by them.
- Examples:

Feelings have a beginning, middle and an end!
Sometimes THE MIDDLE STINKS!

I can't change the past, but I can create my present and build my future.

Feelings can't hurt me, what I do with them can help me or hurt me.

If you always do what you've always done, you'll always get what you always got!

Do not stand in a place of danger and expect miracles. Confucius

---

A Lesson about Self-Injury Behaviors & Thinking: Important Facts

What is Self-Destructive Behavior and Thinking?

Definition

This behavior is called many names, including self-injury, cutting, self-mutilation and para-suicide. Most recently, it has been termed Nonsuicidal self-injury or NSSI. One definition is, "the intentional destruction of body tissue without suicidal intent and for purposes not socially sanctioned" (Klonsky & Muehlenkamp, 2007). This means that the person purposefully harms their own body without intending to die, and that this behavior is not socially sanctioned, such as piercing or tattooing.

Self-injurious behavior also includes to *thinking*. The thoughts tend to be powerful, reflecting strong desires to be in control, to express something, and to try to override the emotions. So, thinking can be very distorted and based more on emotions and feelings than on facts. Thinking like this can cause the state of the body to become very tense and seem overwhelmed. Where the mind goes, so does the body. Tension, anxiety, anger, feeling overwhelmed and fearful can be a terribly suffocating way to feel, and the person just wants it to end and to be back in some sort of control. This is a set of behaviors, thinking and feelings. This is where *intention* comes into consideration. Our thoughts are tied to our behaviors, reactions and feelings. Often when the person changes their behavior, the thoughts and feelings remain unchanged. This is something that therapists want you to understand: *self-destructive behavior is only part of the problem, and is only part of what will need to change.*

Please don't call people by their behaviors, that is, "cutter." Once an identity is formed around such a label, it is hard to change self-definition. It removes the idea that there is ability to control or change behavior.

Self-Destructive Behaviors and Thoughts

Nonsuicidal self-injury can include any number of behaviors or patterns of behaviors, including ritual self-harm. These behaviors can include cutting, burning, scratching, carving, and insertion of objects under the skin. It can also include eating, drinking or swallowing non-food items. There can also be high-risk behaviors such as starvation, drug use, jumping out of moving cars, sexual activities and fighting.

Along with these behaviors are negative and self-destructive thoughts. It is important to understand that our *thinking colors the way we see and respond to the world.* It isn't always accurate or realistic. In addition, our body responds to our thoughts. If you've ever had the experience of being very angry, think about the state of your body. You probably were tense and ready to battle. Over time, the body becomes very able to respond in a way the mind and feelings don't know yet.

Some people have complicated rituals of injury. Sometimes people will go from one type of self-harming behavior to another, such as restricting, binging and throwing up, to cutting, to drug use and sexual acting out.

Sometimes people will pull their eyelashes or hair out compulsively. If this is the only type of self-harm seen, it is important to consider that this may be a form of obsessive-compulsive behavior. If this is the case, then evaluation with someone who specializes in this type of problem is highly recommended.

In some cases, people will also be highly anxious, refuse to go to school or are afraid of school. Their self-injury may help them manage these fears. Again, if this is the case, then evaluation with someone who specializes in this type of problem is highly recommended. Avoidance of school or leaving the home is never recommended, as it may reward the avoidance and fear and actually make it worse.

It is also common to see all sorts of eating disordered behaviors in someone who uses self-injury. Treating both problems is important. The same goes for substance abuse. If the therapist treating your or your family suggests treatment for these problems, listen to them and follow their recommendations. These behaviors are used to help manage feelings and are unhealthy *patterns* of behavior, they all are used to help manage, but not in a healthy way.

Who self-injures?
Depending which study you read, between 13.9% (Ross et al., 2008) of people in the community, up to 50% of teenagers and 35% of college students have admitted they have injured themselves (Gratz, 2001; Lloyd-Richardson et al., 2007; Nock et al., 2007, Whitlock et al., 2006). Even once people seek therapy, many people don't tell their therapist about the behaviors. In a study of college students, only 21% ever talked about to a counselor (Whitlock, Eckenrode & Silverman, 2006). This highlights the importance of asking about the self-injurious behavior and thinking directly.

Why?...or even better HOW is it helpful?
It is hard to think about self-destructive behaviors and thinking can be *helpful*. The behavior has a PURPOSE in that it helps the person manage. It can help the person manage their feelings and thought, or as they will tell you, how it feels "inside" their body and head. So it can help them feel alive (increasing the ability to think and feel), or help them numb it (quieting or decreasing the intensity) (Brown, Comtois, & Linehan, 2002; Nock & Kessler, 2006; Suyemoto, 1998). Another reason is to release tension (Andover, Pepper, Ryabchenko, Orrico, & Gibb, 2005). Some studies have reported that this can help them stop bad feelings, feel alive, and to communicate with other people (Nock & Kessler, 2006).

Simply put, self-destructive behaviors can be thought of serving at least one of four functions (Nock & Cha, 2009):
- To generate feelings, usually from a very numb or empty state
- To escape or lessen bad or negative feelings or thoughts
- To get attention or something from other people or relationships
- To avoid or escape from demands

It is important to make a statement about *seeking attention*. Remember that it is a good thing when people we care about want our attention. This is a very easy thing to address. If someone is so wanting of your attention, think about ways to help this happen. If someone is using self-injury to get your attention, the worse thing you can do is punish them. It is reasonable to expect that people want your attention, but if they want your attention, *they need to use appropriate ways of getting it*. That being said, you must be open to giving them positive attention for positive and age-appropriate behaviors.

Many people immediately think that something terrible must have happened to make someone do this behavior. Actually, that tends not to be true for most people. It is a good question to ask. However, there is a bigger issue. Family conflict and fighting with parents is a common reason given for younger adolescents, and problems with close friends and girl/boyfriends for older adolescents and young adults (Hurry, 2000). The person may not have the ability or maturity to manage these relationships, so understanding both the persons' ability and the influence of the health in both family and social relationships is important. Social skills may not develop evenly. People who self-injure may show some skills in some areas, and not in others, and feel less able to handle situations and problems (Nock & Mendes, 2008).

Lastly, childhood neglect and abuse, family conflict and parental mental health are factors that need to be understood. These cause problems with healthy development and learning skills to manage in relationships in age-appropriate and socially appropriate ways. Learning how to live in the world begins at home. Every person living in the child's home teaches the child something about how to live in the world. Children are great observers, and often do not know what they are seeing, but they are learning the rules of life from watching their families and the people in their lives.

How it is different from suicide and why get help
It is important to understand that the person may be suicidal or have suicidal thoughts, but the purpose of the behavior is TO STAY ALIVE. Self-injury behavior and thinking is a paradoxical behavior, it is used to stay alive. The goal of suicide is to die.

People who self-injure tend to have problems with managing the real and perceived demands of daily living, even if they are doing well in one or more areas. Even if they can problem solve and manage some social situations, they may not be able to manage everyone equally as well. This means the person may be a great student, but injure to manage their feeling that everyone believes they have to be perfect. They probably need professional support even if they say they can control it, or "it happened only once" or it is just a minor injury. In one study, they found that almost 25% of people who have injured will be seen again by medical professionals for injuring within a year; and about 4% of die by suicide within 5-10 years (Beenewith, Stocks, Gunnell, Peters, Evans & Sharp, 2002).

While it is hard to understand, these behaviors and thoughts help people stay alive and manage their feelings and relationships. Current studies suggest that more than half (52.9%) reported they use the behavior to "stop bad feelings" and not to die (Nock & Kessler, 2006). Further studies have shown that suicidal individuals who self-injure typically make suicide attempts during periods of time when they are not using self-injury to manage (Gratz, 2006). It is important to understand what the purpose of the behavior is to the purpose. *"How is it helpful?"* is a much more useful question than *"why did you do it?"*

Are there other problems too?

It is very common that someone who engages in self-injury also has other mental health problems. One study suggested that up to 99% of people who self-injure have some kind of mental health problem (Isacsson & Rich, 2001). In studies looking at teens in an inpatient hospital setting, 61% have a history of self-injury (Nock & Prinstein, 2004). The most common problems appear to be anxiety, depression, post-traumatic stress, eating disorders, substance abuse, anger management, problems with authority, antisocial behaviors, poor self-esteem and impulsivity (Isacsson & Rich, 2001; Jacobsen & Gould, 2007; Nock , Holmberg, Photos & Michel, 2007).

About changing the behavior and thinking patterns

This pattern of thinking, feeling and acting is very difficult to change. This is especially true if the person has been using self-injury to cope for a very long time, or if the person has been using a set of behaviors, like eating disorders, cutting, drugs and sex.

One of the first steps in changing the behavior pattern is the understanding that it serves a purpose (Nock & Prinstein, 2004, 2005; Suyemoto, 1998). This is difficult to accept, especially if you don't understand it. The goal is to help the person develop other healthier ways to manage coping, problem-solving and living their life. This involves "sitting-through" feelings and not acting on them. It also involves willingness to try new things, and create new patterns of behavior, even when the immediate outcome doesn't make the person feel immediately "better." Learning to think through the problem instead of reacting emotionally is important. Likewise, learning a new language and set of skills to communicate thoughts and feelings is important.

Work with your therapist as your guide; don't do this alone. You may be very strong, but this is new territory. Work with honesty and integrity. Honesty involves telling the truth to others. Integrity means working with honesty with yourself. Work cooperatively with your therapist through this process. Consider the values that are discussed in this workbook as your framework and foundation for your recovery.

Read this handbook and seriously think about the information that is presented here. Most people are honestly trying to do the best they can, and would never intentionally try to hurt another person. If you are one of the people, please read this book as helping build off those good intentions.

Recovery involves addressing the mind, the body, the environment and relationships. This book is not written to criticize, judge or shame anyone. People are complicated, and relationships are complicated. Please read these pages as offering you something new to think about and offering you a new way to think about your relationship. At this point parents, family members, support people and you often think about how inconvenient change is, and that their routine "works" for them and their family. This is an opportunity to review just how healthy the family is, and whether or not the convenience and patterns cause health to be neglected. If your kid can't find health in your home, where will they ever learn it? If you can't attempt to be healthy in your own home, then you need to seriously reconsider if it is good for you to be there. You have to practice being healthy in each relationship and in each place you go.

Lastly, understand that there may need to be some serious changes in your home, with how you and your family live with and relate to each other. Anyone living in the home influences any other person there. If you are an adult living in a home with a child, whether you are the parent or not, you are a role model to that child. There may need to be some very difficult changes made about household rules, responsibilities and privileges. Children and teens often know more than they let on. If you as adult isn't healthy, you are modeling your behavior. You change your behavior, the course of the health in your home changes too.

If you are a teenage or young adult living in a house with someone who isn't healthy, you may need to figure out how to be healthy and keep yourself safe until you can be on your own. This is a very sad situation that does happen. You can love people and still be sad and disappointed; this is something to grieve through. Destroying yourself because of what someone did to you, or because someone can't or won't be who you need them to be, is not the answer. You may need to change how you relate to them.

If the treatment team has suggested medication, think about it, ask about it, and do research about it. Get a second opinion. Many of these problems have a biological basis. Would you try to treat cancer or diabetes "naturally"? Would you try to correct your blurry vision or headaches "naturally" if they interfered with your life? The medications might be helpful to assist in the therapy process. However, if medication is used, it is not a cure-all to the problem. Medication can help make the biology of the body work better.

People often neglect the importance of the biology and healthy body functioning. It is important that people who are trying to be healthy have a healthy diet, healthy eating patterns, and sleeping schedule. In our busy lives, we tend to ignore this and instead do what is convenient. Many of us don't think about or nutrition at all, eating what we prefer or is convenient. We allow our children to stay up on their computers and phones. These are the easiest to fix. Healthy routines allow our bodies to recover and become healthy.

Adults living in a home with a child or teen who self-injure have a great opportunity to help change the life of this person. Likewise, they can bring terrible pain and suffering. If you are an adult reading this because you care about someone who self-injures, please understand your own behavior and live your life speaks volumes more than your words. So if you, the adult in the home abuses substances, has an eating disorder, is involved in an abusive relationship, or has anger management problems, your efforts at changing your patterns will be a first step in bringing the entire family/household into a healthier balance. Being a parent is not easy. Practicing what you preach, and being consistent is necessary.

Another critically important thing is to have limits, expectations, and clear accountability in your relationships. There is more about this later in this book. The message is that to be healthy, one needs to be involved in healthy relationships. Healthy relationships have rules, expectations, limits, and boundaries. They also have rules and, to some extent, a hierarchy. These are based on age and developmentally-appropriate standards. One problem with teens who self-injure, is that far too often, they have many more privileges than they have the emotional maturity to manage. In addition, they have little understanding of responsibility, and expect that they can have what they want with little effort. This will also be covered in this book.

Understand that people who are giving up a pattern of self-injury struggle, and often feel worse before they get better. That is why therapy and support can be so helpful; it gets everyone through the tough times. Sometimes, the behavior relapses, and that does not mean the person failed or that therapy failed. This is something to talk about *with the therapist*.

This journal is for people who struggle with both self-destructive behaviors and thinking. At times, you may struggle to the extent that you are suicidal. What many people don't understand is that self-destructive behaviors are often used *to stay alive*. This journal is written to help you begin to think differently about self-destructive patterns in your life. It is for people who are willing to stay alive.

It is recommended to work with a therapist while working through this journal. Believe it or not, many people who self-injure never tell their therapist about their self-injury. One aspect of being healthy is to be honest and open with your therapist about your self-injury history and behaviors. Therapy is about helping you manage, problem-solve and develop healthier ways to manage your feelings, thoughts and impulses.

There are several important concepts to learn, and so it is important to read the lessons. Every thing in the journal has a purpose and meaning. The change you want to make is a really big one, and working in little pieces at a time is important. There are several important things to know about self-destructive behaviors:

1. The behaviors serve a purpose. The purpose may not be as helpful or long-lasting in relief. It can serve as expression, release, punishment, translation of pain, just to name a few of the functions. Another reason is to communicate with someone, and attempt to connect with another person.
2. For some people, self-injury is used to stay alive. The goal of suicide is to die. Sometimes people have both ideas at the same time. People with suicidal thoughts who self-injure may make more suicide attempts when they are not using self-destructive behaviors.
3. Self-destructive thinking can be just as problematic as the behavior. It can color how one sees and responds to the world.
4. Asking someone how self-destructive behaviors are helpful is a great question. It doesn't matter if you (the person asking the question) agree or support it; it helps to understand it that is the persons' perspective of how much the person is struggling.
5. The goal of treatment is to develop alternative healthy coping skills for the person to CHOOSE to use. Unfortunately we (therapists, parents) can't make them make certain choices. We (therapists, parents) can provide consistent support, structure and logical consequences for unhealthy decisions and behaviors.
6. Self-injury serves as a way to take the intensity inside and express it externally.
7. These behaviors can become a like a habit, used to manage feelings and thoughts or to communicate. However, these habits can ultimately cause loss of independence and cause serious health problems.
8. These behaviors interfere with taking care of ones self in a developmentally appropriate way. Other age-appropriate healthy ways of soothing, calming or managing don't develop.
9. These behaviors change the physiology of ones body. This means that the person becomes more and more sensitive and avoidant of feelings, or become more easily triggered into using self-destructive behaviors.

10. Because of using these behaviors, it is difficult to recognize unhealthy patterns and behaviors of others. This makes it harder to make better choices about how you manage relationships with other people.

11. Sometimes people have a number of different unhealthy behaviors, and rotate through them. The most common ones tend to be self-injury, eating disorders, substance use, and high risk behaviors.

12. The most common reasons causing self-injury tends to be conflict, relationship problems, chaos, inconsistency and fighting. Interestingly, these are common problems in adolescence, but the person doesn't have the developmental maturity and often lacks the support of healthy parents and role models to provide structure, limits, and skills manage these demands. The social peer group may be part of the problem. However, when there is a child or teenager with a problem, there is a family element that needs to be addressed too.

13. Some families can't or won't provide the emotional or physical support that a child or teen needs. Addressing that, grieving that, and finding other ways of getting support is important.

14. Learning physical relaxation techniques, like T'ai Chi, progressive relaxation, yoga, and mediation are very important tools to help teach the mind and body to work together. This is why we teach the deep breathing technique and encourage people to practice it throughout the day.

15. You must be willing to treat this problem holistically: mind, body, and spirit.

Structure in recovery from problems with self-injury behaviors and thoughts is very important. When things are scary, new or different, knowing the structure is the most important thing to keep you on track. The structure is built on your VALUES and your GOALS, and serves as the Framework for Recovery. This Framework is your guide when you struggle.

1. Throughout the journal, you will see different sayings, quotes, and opportunities for you to create your own flashcards. Use these as a reference to help you when you feel overwhelmed or lost. When you have to make a hard decision, go back to your values and your daily goal, and make a decision in your own best interest (Safety, Security, and Physical Well-Being).
2. Don't make decisions based on what you want, but on what you need (your own best interest).
3. It is important to have a working relationship with your therapist that is based on honesty, accountability, cooperation and tolerance of feelings is important. This also means disclosure about injury, self-care, and high risk behaviors, suicidal ideation, intent or behavior.
4. In your therapeutic relationship, and your significant relationships in life, it is important to have a working relationship that has limits, expectations for healthy choices, and logical consequences built into the structure are important.
5. Logical consequences are *not* the same as punishment. They are what happens after something, and can be positive or negative. I would never support punishment for self-injury. A logical consequence of injuring should be a referral to a physician or nurse for wound care. A logical consequence of failing to sustain weight or losing weight, if the individual is on a meal plan, may be referral back to an appropriate level of care such as inpatient or partial hospital. It means having limits and a mechanism that provides external structure when the individual either is not able to or won't manage in an age-appropriate and healthy way. Every healthy relationship needs reasonable and age-appropriate structure and limits.
6. We do not discuss details of injury, especially in a group setting. It is appropriate to state, "I self-injured," but not discuss the exact *how* of injury in group. This helps keep the focus on the choice to harm and not on the details and how to injure. It also helps keep competition down and lessons on how to injure minimized. Further, it helps avoid some very graphic and explicit details, and decreases the shock value to the group.
7. It is important to include discussions about values, purpose and meaning of life. The next step is building into the conversation the importance of this belief system as the guidepost for making decisions about how one behaves in the world, has relationships with self and others.
8. It is also important to see these behaviors as choices that people make versus who they are. These are people who self-injure, they are their symptoms. They are not "*cutters*," "*burners*," or "*starvers*." As therapists, we do not want our patients identifying with their symptoms and using these behaviors as the foundation of self-definition. Our self-definition becomes our foundation for how we interact with the world.

9. It is important to look at self-definition versus self-esteem. Self-esteem can be used as an excuse to avoid being responsible. For example, "she does this because she has poor self-esteem." How one defines oneself is far more important than how one values oneself. We have value or worth because of being alive; it is what we do with our lives and how we live our lives that gives us value. Discussing self-esteem is just a great way to engage in a power struggle that everyone loses. You'll never win a power-struggle with someone arguing over their self-esteem. As a therapist, I say to people, "you have value, deal with it; how you live your life tells others how you value yourself."

10. Avoid power struggles. Therapy has known predictable limits. There are known logical consequences when that limit is not met, there are expectations and accountability built into these limits. When someone can't or won't self-manage within those expectations and limits, the logical consequences built into the structure should be imposed. Period. No negotiations. I don't negotiate with terrorists or people who can self-manage. This is the foundation of any healthy parenting, and for that matter, all healthy relationships. It is important that this philosophy is brought into the home as well. Family relationships need known predictable limits and structure too. Often times people give in to power struggles which helps create an "emotional terrorist" and this ends up not teaching people the rules of appropriate behavior, healthy communication and tolerance for frustration. These are IMPORTANT and NECESSARY skills for living successfully in the world.

11. A foundation for developing self-management is built upon the idea that *privileges are earned*, not given. Self-sufficiency is developed through skill building, being held accountable, and then being given some form of positive consequence. For example, when a child begins to brush their teeth on their own consistently, the parent can back off and not check, but ask occasionally.

12. All too often in our society, what once was a privilege is now something that everyone has, and one doesn't have to work too hard for anything. For example, children assume they will have a computer, designer clothes, and cell phones. No longer are these earned. It is not uncommon to see parents punishing their children for self-injury, so they take the cell phone away. This doesn't help healthy self-management and sets up power struggles over the item instead of being a logical consequence for poor self-management and poor choices.

13. Privileges should be age appropriate and based on ability to manage in an age-appropriate manner. When there are privileges without ability to manage that privilege, it is a set-up for problems. Privileges evolve and develop as the individual is able to manage.

14. Consistency is important. A limit is a limit. Accountability is important.

15. The goal of relationships, whether these are child-parent or therapist-client, is not one of equality in terms of responsibility. These are relationships that have a goal of helping mentor, teach and shape the child/patient to develop healthy self-management, within age-appropriate structure, accountability and limits.

16. Healthy conflict is a necessary part of healthy development. Conflict is a normal and necessary part of life and relationships. When parents don't model healthy ways of managing frustration, anger, conflict resolution and limit setting, their children don't learn it.

17. Many times parents are inconsistent with their rules and limits. This sends very conflicting messages to their children. Further, many parents want to avoid conflict because of the intensity, emotions and fear of making their children unhappy. Consequently, these children can't tolerate anger, frustration and authority. Therapy may involve a great deal of conflict, and may involve bringing the family in to the process.

18. Remember that actions speak loudly. Words and actions, when they send the same message, are the best teachers.

19. Emotions can be difficult to manage, especially if maturity and language skills are lacking. Part of treatment involves learning new and healthy ways of self-expression and getting needs met.

20. Everyone should be able to save face, to be able to admit when they've made a poor choice or bad decision. Asking people what they've learned and what they hope to accomplish, and exploring other options is important.

21. Create opportunities to look for a range of options in choices.

22. Create opportunities to think about things differently.

23. People do better when they know what the expectations and limits are, and the consequences (costs and benefits) of their choices.

24. Kids need parents to be parents and teachers and therapists to be healthy mentors. Parents who parent through fear of making their child unhappy are not able to help their child learn healthy self-management.

25. The goal of recovery, and of life, is to create health, and ability to manage self. The goal of parenting is to raise self-sufficient and healthy children. The goal of life and parenting is not to make people happy. Happiness is a by-product of the way we live our lives.

26. Treating self-injury and self-destructive behavior is not just about the injury. It is about creating the ability to self-manage and make other choices. It is about understanding that behavior and thinking patterns have purpose, and that developing other behaviors to choose from and meet needs is important.

27. It is important to create and foster hope. Believing that people are capable of being different, can manage their feelings and thoughts is critical.

28. Getting help, needing support and guidance is not weakness. Anyone who gives that message is inaccurate and not helpful. No one would do open heart surgery on themselves or stop the progression of cancer, or expect an infant to teach themselves to use the toilet alone. Face it, we all need support and mentoring. Those who are connected to other people who are healthy, supportive and mentoring; and expecting that we can become healthy humans; are those we need in our lives.

29. Yes it is hard to change, but you can become the change you want, the person you want to become. Every day is a new opportunity. Learn from your lapses, get up when you fall, own it, learn from it, then do something about it!

- It is about the thinking, feeling, conclusions and relationships you have with yourself and with the world, than it is about the behavior.
- It involves change.
- It involves changing how we relate to ourselves, our body, other people, and the world around us.
- It involves choosing different behaviors and beliefs.
- It involves learning to tolerate feelings.
- It involves willingness to have values.
- It involves being willing to see yourself as having worth and value, and being worthy of self-respect.
- It involves your commitment to practicing being safe, secure and physically well.
- It involves managing thinking, feeling, and relationships you have with yourself and with the world, so that the choices around behavior are different.
- It is about creating options for managing your emotional intensity, either to help tolerate feelings, decrease them or learn to allow them to be present.

So to answer the question about what you can do:
- Understand that the behavior is only one part of the problem. It also involves the thinking, feeling and reacting.
- Understand that the behavior serves a function or purpose.
- Understand that self-injury is not the same as suicide.
- Understand the recommendations made by professionals.
- Understand that there are real mental health problems involved here.
- People who self-injure are people with problems staying alive and coping.
- They are not their problems or their behavior; that is, people are not "cutters."
- People who self-injure can rotate through symptoms. If the underlying problem doesn't change, the behavior may rotate through different phases.
- Understand that the process of change takes time.
- Accept that there may need to be some changes in your own household.
- Accept that you may need to change the way you interact or deal with the person.
- Consider the importance of healthy limits, boundaries and expectations as a foundation for health.
- Understand the importance of taking care of the whole body, the whole person.
- You will have to consider how you relate to people, and your friends, family and other relationships.
- You may have to consider changing activities and patterns.
- It involves active, honest, and consistent participation in treatment.
- Be willing to live with values, and make decisions based on those that you CHOOSE to make important.
- Allow your therapist to be your guide during the process.
- Accept responsibility for your choices.
- Problem-solve and think your way through recovery; let your goals and values be your guide.

- Feelings are not facts, they tell you something important is going on.
- You can choose your behaviors and reactions.
- Behaviors show true intentions, not words.
- You can tolerate feelings; it is the behaviors you choose that make them "dangerous."
- No one ever died because of their feelings.
- You are the most powerful person in your life. Deal with that fact!

The BASICS involve managing your internal world, interactions with external world and your physical well-being.

- Safety refers to managing the *internal processes* related to managing your thoughts, feelings and actions. It involves being aware of your experiences in the present and being connected. This is your thinking, your feelings and reactions. It is your "inside" world.
- Security refers to the *interaction between the external world and yourself* and the *processes related to how you make decisions about relationships with people, places and things in your life.* This involves the relationships between you and your world.
- Physical Well-Being involves how you go about managing your decisions and actions related to self-care, nutrition, medication, sleep hygiene/rest, etc. It involves being connected to and respectful of, your physical body and well-being. This is the relationship you have with your body and your "self."

To make change work over time, it is important that your behaviors be consistent, fit your plan and make sense, fitting your goals. For your plan to establish healthy self-management using the *BASICS* needs to include:

- CONSISTENCY – in your plan, approach or framework. Your choices and action need to be consistent, even if it doesn't get the desired outcome at first or if it is difficult.

  CONSISTENCY: evenness, sameness, reliable, constant
- CONGRUITY – your plan, approach or framework has to FIT you, your goals and desired outcome. Your plan, choices and actions, should be congruent with what you want to create for yourself.

  CONGRUENCE: similarity, equivalence
- COHERENT – the plan, approach or frame must make SENSE to you related to maintaining your BASICS and attaining your desired goals

  COHERENT: reasonable, sound, rational, logical

The CHANGE ACTIONS are the focus for all changes. When you have focus, direction, determination and commitment, the behavioral components of your plan become much more possible to reach. They help you THINK your way through your decisions, think your way through your impulses and feelings. These set your attitude and mindset, helping you be mindful about what it is you are trying to accomplish, and where you are trying to go in your recovery process. Defining these components for yourself helps you be very clear and focused on your desired goals and to help determine your behaviors (choices).

Focus:	Ability to pay attention and prioritize your efforts
Direction:	Focused purposeful effort of your thoughts and behaviors towards a specific desired outcome. Knowing what you need & being willing to work towards it.
Determination:	Finding a way to stay focused, on task and making it work. Knowing what you need and moving towards it. Making hard

	choices and keeping your eye on your goal, especially when it is hard.
Commitment:	Committed to maintaining your safety, security and physical well-being. It is an investment in yourself and your desired goals.

The *Foundation Skills*:

The foundation of your recovery involves several components that are based on your self definition and operating principles.

Communication:	Information exchange with others, interaction and self talk
Collaboration:	Working with your treatment providers by taking an active role, working towards agreed upon goals; working as a partnership
Cooperation:	Willingness to work with your treatment providers, working actively towards to accomplish your agreed upon goals
Connectedness:	Understanding that recovery has to be a part of what you are, a part of everything you are doing and working towards in recovery

Student of Self:

- Paying attention to opportunities to learn about yourself, your life, and the people, places and things around you
- Being aware of the lessons, learning from your choices, putting together the connection between choices, actions and outcomes
- Being open and aware of information around you and how you can change your reactions to your world
- This is an attitude involving openness, willingness and taking in new information, learning from experiences

---

All of life is a constant education.
People grow through experience if they meet life honestly and courageously.
This is how character is built.
Eleanor Roosevelt

Psychological Position:

This is the attitude or <u>POSITION</u> that is an active psychological role you take as you go through every moment of every day. It involves how you think about and react to your world.

- A mindful psychological position one takes in their life
- It involves HOW you approach your life, how you think about your life
    - That means are you:
        - Reactive, emotional and avoidant?
        - Explosive?
        - Sensitive, passive, accepting responsibility for things that aren't yours?
        - Always expecting others to punish or hurt you?
        - Someone who uses self-injury to avoid the pain that you think is coming?
- In this framework one take a *psychological position or role* to interact with their life as a *Victim* or *Survivor*. This is a MINDFUL choice you CAN make.

- Victim Position: Reactive, passive, sees only limited range of options, gives authority away, makes decisions based on "wants", doesn't tolerate feelings
- Survivor Position: Active, proactive, generates range of options, owns authority for self, makes decisions based on "needs" and "goals," tolerates feelings, uses THINKING and self-management of reactions
- *You can choose how you react.* It involves thinking your way through your world, being open to new information.
- Taking a psychological SURVIVOR POSITION means:
  - Thinking about what is happening around you.
  - Recognizing patterns around you.
  - Tolerating feelings, they tell you something is important; AND then using your thinking and keeping your eye on your goal.
  - Accepting responsibility for your actions, choices and decisions.
  - KNOWING WHERE YOU ARE GOING AND WHAT YOU WANT
  - Making goal and value based decisions, and having your behavior match (congruency).
  - Actively making decisions that are in your own best interest and help you make it to your daily goal.
  - Learning from your experiences, being a student of yourself and the world around you.
  - Being mindful, aware and connected in your present.
  - Taking an active role in your life.

Pattern Recognition:

It is important to be aware of patterns and collecting data about your life. Data involves looking at the real facts and outcomes, not just using internal "feeling" based ones. Recognizing patterns and the way that they connect to lead to specific behaviors, feelings or outcomes is important. Once patterns are identified, it becomes easier to identify ways to change patterns. This change is called *Pattern Recognition.*

Even when you believe you can never change existing patterns or that things will never be different, it is important to keep your eye on your desired goal and behave as though things can be different. Interrupting automatic feelings is just as important as interrupting automatic reactions, behaviors and choices. It is important to recognize opportunities to practice new behavioral patterns.

It is important to think about experiences in terms of links on a chain. For example, first this happens, then this, then that….and then the outcome or ending. Each link is an important part of the chain. You can manage to interrupt patterns, and it may be very uncomfortable. You can manage to chose to manage yourself, limit the use of symptomatic behaviors and change aspects of your life that you are in charge of, such as your thoughts, behaviors, feelings and reactions.

Framework for Recovery:

This is your road map for change and your path to keep you focused, and structure for when you get lost. The <u>Contract with Myself</u> is one of the foundations of your Framework for Recovery. This is why goals, focus, determination and values are important.

VALUES

Values are necessary to help you have a healthy Framework to use in decision making. Values are something you can choose to adopt. They help you define who you are, and what you define as important to you. This foundation is necessary for guiding goals, your choices and actions:

Dignity	Self respect, honoring yourself
Honesty	Telling the truth to others, honoring the truth
Integrity	Telling the truth to yourself, honoring your own truth
Respect	Having honor towards oneself and others
Responsibility	Having investment in owning what you commit to accomplishing
Accountability	Being willing to be responsible to commitments made
Willingness	Being open to trying new options or choices, motivation to be different
Openness	Being willing to be willing to try new options or choices
Tolerance	Being willing to put up with feeling or thoughts that are uncomfortable or new
Boundaries	Having healthy limits, respecting ones personal space
Patience	Endurance over a long period of time, keeping your eye on the future
Awareness	Having knowledge about experiences, reactions and thoughts
Mindfulness	Being aware of choices, reactions, and being present in the moment
Empathy	Having understanding and sympathy
Kindness	Being gentle and benevolent
Compassion	Having consideration, empathy and benevolence with another
Perseverance	Having determination and endurance towards something important
Cooperation	Aligning yourself with your goal and acting in your best interest

NOTE: This is the part where people often say something like "I don't deserve this" or some other negative self-talk. Here is something to think about:

> You can decide you are worth it and deserve it. You may seriously need to reconsider that you give away your value when you do this. *This is an opportunity to try something new.*

No one is ready to work on very deep and emotional issues, such as trauma or abuse, if they can't or won't:

- Keep safe and physically well
- Stay grounded and connected to the present
- Tolerate having feelings
- Maintain a safety plan and know when to ask for help
- Be honest about their intentions
- Work cooperatively with their treatment team
- Be willing, honest, tolerant, courageous

> *You gain strength, courage, and confidence by each experience in which you really stop to look fear in the face.*

> *You are able to say to yourself, I have lived through this horror.*

> I can take the next thing that comes along. You must do the thing you think you cannot do.
>
> *No one can make you feel inferior without your consent. Eleanor Roosevelt*
>
> Remember always that you not only have the right to be an individual, you have an obligation to be one. Eleanor Roosevelt

At this point in your recovery process, a good starting point needs to be on STRUCTURING your focus and your daily activities.

- Having a goal serves as a guiding beacon, a light guiding you towards your desired destination. In recovery, our decisions and behaviors should fit (be congruent with) our goals.
- How you manage your feelings, thinking and actions are the foundations of MINDFULNESS and AWARENESS in managing your present and all choices you make.
- You can take a psychological survivor position and actively manage your life.
- This involves being aware that you have a choice in how you react to your world, managing your feelings and reactions. This helps to manage your thoughts and stay present in the here and now.
- One important starting point is the emphasis on AFFECT (feelings) TOLERANCE, not avoidance, and working on decreasing the intensity of your reactions.

> *Do not dwell in the past, do not dream of the future, concentrate the mind on the present moment. Buddha*

There are cases and problems that tend to cause therapists to step back and think twice about engaging in a therapeutic relationship. These tend to be centered on high risk, suicidal, impulsive and /or destructive problems. The following section is designed to address a number of issues to help therapists have a different perspective on managing these types of problems within a one to one therapeutic relationship. This section is written from the perspective of my own training and experiences. For further theoretical foundation, please refer to the works of John Levitt, Ph.D. (2004). This is my foundation and the way I think my way through the process:

APPROACH/POSITION to treatment:
- There is no negotiation with or about Safety, Security and Physical Well-Being.
- Decisions and feedback are made on EVIDENCE or DATA, not intentions or effort.
- Imposed therapeutic structure has to be at the level the patient/family is functioning.
- Therapy is not PERSONAL to me. The presenting problems are not mine; therefore there is no reason to ever respond personally. Asking, "how do you want me to respond to that?" is a great modeling question. It demonstrates that I can choose how to respond/react; and it allows them the opportunity to tell you what they want. You can then respond reasonably and appropriately.
- People don't have to "prove" anything to me. This is especially true about trust. Saying "Why should I believe you?" puts us both into a power struggle. Saying "What is the evidence that your words and behaviors will be congruent?" (ok translate that to people-speak), is far more accurate. "How do you know you will be safe?" "How will you know if you are becoming overwhelmed?" "What is the data about your safety?"
- Don't try to cover too much ground at one time.
- If people can't keep themselves safe, it isn't time to be talking about memories of trauma. Timing and pacing is everything.
- My role as the therapist is:
  - Guide/teacher of the process
  - Be the "holder" of:
    - Expectations and Accountability
    - Containment and Structure
    - Pacing, timing and intensity
  - Be the "reminder" of:
    - What is the desired outcome or goal
    - Values guiding the decision making process
    - Options to achieve the desired goal or outcome
    - Opportunities to try something new occur every moment
    - They are going to need to try something new pretty often
    - What the consequences or outcomes are for the decision options
    - Rules, obligations and expectations
    - Responsibilities appropriate to age and developmental capacities

- Healthy relationships
- What is "reasonable" and "unreasonable"
- Pointing out the obvious inconsistencies, incongruities and outcomes, and asking if the "WHEN…THEN…" connections are what is desirable.
- Being direct, honest and containment
- Interact based on the expectation that the individual can manage their own life without self-injury or other self-destructive behaviors.
- Our goal is to provide structure, contain, interrupt patterns and redirect or create opportunities for new healthier patterns.
- Our role is to teach new strategies for using information (both internal and external), recognize patterns of managing thoughts and feelings, and practice using new strategies, collecting data, and bringing it back to re-evaluate how well it is working.
- Therapy should be about establishing:
  - Establishing safety, or the ability to self-manage thoughts, feelings and choices about their behaviors; in the context of what they are trying to achieve, and in reference to what outcomes are generated by their behaviors.
  - Recognizing patterns of how they use the behaviors and when they use them.
  - Recognition of internal states (i.e., being overwhelmed, or trying to numb out), and how to manage tolerating affect and staying connected.
  - Understanding the purpose or function of the behavior, and generating other ways to meet those needs.
- Structuring the process of discussing the content. This means structuring what content material is discussed, and assuring that the process of discussing them is always about how they are managing themselves in the discussion. Any content material should always be discussed from the perspective of how the person can self-manage (as above) while they are trying to manage the issues in their life.
- As a therapist, it is also important to have an agenda that is based in establishing safety, security and physical well-being, and basing the process on keeping the patient focused on creating that in their lives. That is our goal; we need to keep coming back to it as part of the structure of treatment. However we often have our own agenda about what we belief the patient should be *talking about,* and miss how they are structuring their own lives and what they need to do to be doing those activities. Back off from your own agenda, and keep to the process of creating the structure and what they need to be creating that safety, security and physical well-being. Until they can consistently self-regulate, these terms need to be constantly used.
  - Think metaphorically, we can't expect a child to brush their teeth independently if we aren't building the skill set to do it. What are the steps in teaching someone these skills? Think about it. What are the words you use as you structure and teach, and repeatedly teach as they become more

self-sufficient? Believe it or not, these skills you the teacher use translate to practice with the patient learning self-regulation:

- Statement of the end result
- Statements of what you are trying to accomplish
- Statements of the purpose or reason
- Identification of helpful behaviors and decisions
- Encouragement for the efforts and achievement
- Acknowledgment of the difficulty
- Observations of goal-directed behaviors

LANGUAGE USED & TALKING TOO MUCH:

Language is important. How we use language is also important. Clarifying *meaning* is a critical aspect of teaching language and conceptualization for expression and skill attainment. Break things down, don't talk AT them.

- Asking *how* they understand what is being said is important. "What did you hear me say?" is a great question. Engage them. Understand they may not respond.
- Most of the conversation should take the form of Socratic questions and exploring cause/effect and recognizing patterns and opportunities to try something different.
- We are teaching how to effectively communicate thoughts and feelings and to develop conceptualization around intense feelings and overwhelming thoughts.
- Asking about how they understand or make sense of their world and relationships helps you understand how they understand the rules of life. You can help clarify whether or not their understanding is *distorted, inaccurate* or *unreasonable*.
- We sometimes talk too much and miss the cues that the person isn't listening, isn't able to listen or is affectively and physically overwhelmed.
- "*Suicidal*" and "*like injuring*" are not feelings, they are conclusions about an internal state. Teach your patient the meaning of the words they use. Encourage them to be accurate in their expression and language usage.
- Connecting affect and internal intensity to language constructs is a skill set.
- Connecting appropriate language and developmental capacity is important.

RECOGNIZE THE PHYSICAL CUES:

- This is one of the MOST IMPORTANT areas of intervention in teaching the patient to be safe within themselves (managing their thoughts, feelings and choices about behavior), and secure or being able to manage their relationship with the outside world (people, places and things).
- This is a real therapeutic opportunity in the moment to teaching your patient about recognizing increasing tension, discomfort or other messages their body is "sending" them that they may not recognize. Don't hesitate to interrupt the content of the conversation to make observations about what their body is telling them.
  - For example you could say, "are you aware of what your body is doing right now?" Then provide them with your observations. Ask them if they are aware of what they might be reacting to or the body-speak is connected to in terms of the process/content happening.
  - It is then a moment where you can do some socratic and reflective discussion about mind-body connection.

- It is also an opportunity to practice some mind-body work, like the grounding exercise, breathing, stretching, etc. At this point any education about reasonable reactions and appropriate self-soothing can be very validating and supportive to the person.
- Because some of the function of self-injury can be about managing the internal intensity (i.e., feeling too much or trying to feel something), these people often lack the ability to tolerate the feeling of being in their body. This is a piece of connectedness and being present in the moment that is a critical process to help them learn to manage. Just as when you feel overwhelmed and want to take a break to get some relief from that intensity, that is we try to teach:
  - Recognition that they are overwhelmed or numb.
  - Recognition that they are not connected to the present moment (i.e., inside their heads, disconnected or even dissociated).
  - Recognizing when they are becoming "triggered" or becoming less connected and overwhelmed.
  - Interruption of these patterns before they become too big to handle, and the individual then uses the self-destructive behavior to cope.
- Interrupt escalation of affect or being overwhelmed with a physical activity.
- Stand up, breathe, and use grounding exercises to interrupt physical escalation.
- Reflect to them the observations you see. "May I tell you what I am seeing?" "Are you aware that your body is…." "What is your body telling you?"
- CONNECT mind and body through stretching, breathing, and moving.
- Teach physical state awareness and connection. Recommend practicing relaxation 3-5 times a day. Practice when they are not overwhelmed or at risk.
- Connecting parasympathetic (relaxation) skills to stimulation (sympathetic) is important. You can't be both simultaneously.
- Pay attention for when your patient is at that wall. Interrupt the pattern of being overwhelmed with physical stretches, breathing, and standing if necessary.

CHOICE & PERSONAL RESPONSIBILITY:
- The goal of therapy is to help the person become able to THINK their way through their life (real and perceived demands, problems, situations) and to make decisions based on THEIR BEST INTERESTS (which is managing one's Safety, Security and Physical Well-Being appropriately for their age and developmental level).
- People are responsible for their actions. They are responsible for being grounded and connected, and they are responsible for their actions when/if they dissociate. These are two important working rules for our patients.
- We are building an *internal locus of control* or ownership for their feelings, reactions and thoughts. Even though things happen to us that we have no control over, we are in control of how we react to them, the decisions we make and the actions we take. This is a psychological position that is active and proactive.
- The person, as a result of their choices and actions, "earns" or comes into a set of consequences. Let's define that word. Consequences are costs/benefits or outcomes of behaviors. They can be desirable or undesirable. They can be logical or natural outcomes. You, the therapist, do not experience the consequence. Your obligation is to

have stated, known expectations and limits, and discuss them and the plan of action if needed. This is your containment and stated parameter.

- Because I, the therapist, do not experience the consequence, and the problem is not mine, I can remain neutral and act as a guide/teacher to the person, at least until the parameters of safety and physical well-being are compromised and I act according to these known parameters.
- People do not have to choose to be healthy. They can un-choose it and decide to be unhealthy. The therapists' obligation is to then decide to move the person to the next level of care, or to un-choose working with the patient if the relationship no longer has the goal of working towards creating health and safety.
- Avoid power struggles. No one ever wins a power struggle, and no one wants to be a loser. Therefore people, when pushed into a battle, will often make choices to "win" over losing. Every one must have the option of saving face.

AFFECT MANAGEMENT:
- Sometimes it is not important to recognize *what* the feeling state is, but that it *exists* and *how big* is it. This is because recognizing the increase or decrease of internal intensity is an important self-management skill.
- Feelings are not facts, feelings tell us something important is happening, and should be used as cues to pay attention to what is going on in the moment.
- When we use feelings as facts, our perceptions are often colored by things that have very little to do with the present moment. We end up responding to something that isn't happening in the moment, and our conclusions and behaviors are often inaccurate.
- The skills or capacities that the therapeutic process fosters regarding affect include:
    - Affect tolerance, recognizing that having intense feelings is difficult, but it is the choices they make that can be dangerous, not the feelings themselves.
        - "Feelings won't hurt you, it is what you do with those feelings that can be dangerous or defeating for you"
        - "Feelings have a beginning, middle and an end. Sometimes the middle stinks!"
    - Recognizing and interrupting maladaptive behaviors used to change internal intensity
    - Recognizing that affect/feelings color one's experiences and ability to take in information about their world.
    - Feelings are not facts, they are information that something important is happening.
    - We have the ability to evaluate situations and influence how we "feel" about them.

The Process of Therapy with Someone with Self-Destructive Behaviors
- It is a *Self-Regulatory Behavior. As long as they are using self-destructive behavior somewhat effectively, why would they use something else?*
- Therapy should be about establishing:
    - Establishing safety, or the ability to self-manage thoughts, feelings and choices about their behaviors; in the context of what they are trying to achieve, and in reference to what outcomes are generated by their behaviors.

- Recognizing patterns of how they use the behaviors and when they use them.
- Recognition of internal states (i.e., being overwhelmed, or trying to numb out), and how to manage tolerating affect and staying connected.
- Understanding the purpose or function of the behavior, and generating other ways to meet those needs.
- Begin by creating structure, which involves clarification of goals based on safety, security and physical well-being and the parameters of the therapeutic relationship.
- Remember to think across a spectrum of behaviors governing functioning: eating, substances, risky, self-destructive, exercising, sleep, etc.
- Clarify expectations and method of holding them accountable for their behaviors.
  - This includes logical consequences (outcomes, responses) for self-destructive behaviors.
    - Wound care, inadequate self-care (sleep, nutrition), substance abuse, and/or high risk behaviors should clearly be identified as needing to be monitored and addressed.
    - Wound care should never be done by the therapist, partly because unless you are a medical professional, you can set up a secondary gain situation. The relationship becomes based on the interaction around the wound and wound care process.
  - This should also include what the parameters are for consideration for a highly level of care. This discussion is important so that they understand what the limits are and so they can decide how to act/behave within those parameters. Therefore, you, the therapist, is not the holder of the decision of when, but you are responsible for upholding the structure and agreed upon response of when the boundaries are violated. This is a subtle but critical use of language and thinking conceptualization. We don't "react" as clinicians, we respond according to the rules of the structure of the relationship. Like with parenting, there is an "IF…THEN…" that is based in logic, clearly stated parameters and boundaries. This line in the sand helps create boundaries and limits, which allows the patient to begin to self-regulate. It also creates an opportunity for them to choose their own behaviors within the context of understanding what the possible outcomes will be. This helps create self-regulation and connect their choices and outcomes of their behaviors to consequences incurred. The perceived randomness of life decreases and more internalization can occur.
  - A discussion about what is their own pattern of self-destructive thinking and behaviors, antecedent/precipitants and sustaining factors is important. This means we have to clarify with our patients what:
    - Their inventory of self-destructive behaviors includes
    - Generally happens before an episode
    - How quickly it escalates to self-destructiveness
    - How much planning goes into the event
    - What maintains it, makes it possible to go back to the behavior
    - What the benefit or purpose of the behavior is to them
  - Lastly, there needs to be a direct discussion about suicide and high risk behaviors and when is "too much" for them to manage alone. This clearly also

sets the parameters for safety and physical well-being, so they know and you know when the next level of care is needed.

- A word on "suicide contracts" is needed. Depending on your perspective, your discipline of practice, your liability and malpractice and attorney and supervisors position, you may be for or against them. In my practice, we contract for life. It is consistent with our goal of entering therapy with the goal of staying alive.

- Clarify and define extent of self-management and difficulties in functioning.
- Teaching self-regulation involves:
  - Increasing tolerance of affect
  - Developing alternative psychological cohesiveness to manage
  - POINTING OUT DISCREPANCIES between words and actions, stated goals and actions
  - Increased ability to delay gratification and manage impulses
  - Increased language and conceptualization abilities
  - Identifying the purpose/function of the behavior and creating a new way to get those needs met
  - Increased internalization, as "IF…THEN…" and connection to choices and behaviors are connected to logical and reasonable consequences and outcomes.
- Encourage the patient to manage in the present, to take in present based data and make decisions based on the present situation, present goals, etc.
- Approach to intervention should be very focused and based in creating a new *structure* for managing (thoughts, decisions, feelings, interaction, actions, and reactions).
- All discussions about behaviors and actions should be in the context of the stated and identified goals of recovery. Use the goal as a POINT OF REFERENCE.
- Focus and direct all actions to HOW things fit together (congruence) in working towards self-management and towards the goal.
- Focus and direct all actions to HOW behaviors (thoughts too) are *helpful*. In defining helpful, this means weighing the costs and the benefits, looking at how the behavior is congruent with goals and values.
- Clarify and anticipate HOW they are going to manage their feelings or impulses. It is about managing and focused effort in the here and now.
- Their job is to manage and tolerate the affect they are experiencing while working on developing alternative healthy coping skills. The patient is in treatment to talk about patterns, external cues/triggers, components and aspects that impact their choices to use self-destructive behaviors versus other management.
  - Definition of TRIGGER is important. Some patients will avoid taking responsibility for their own actions, they'll say, "she triggered me…" It is important to reframe these CUES as things they chose to respond to using a specific set of behaviors. They are responsible for their actions and behaviors.
- The expectations of therapy include:
  - That the patient will work on managing their affect and internal intensity
  - That the patient will manage their behavior in a healthy way
  - That the patient will manage their thinking
  - That the patient will recognize and interrupt patterns of behavior
  - That the patient will work on keeping themselves

- Grounded and connected in the present, and managing their thoughts
- In healthy relationships and safe places with healthy other people
- Engaged in safe and healthy activities
- Will take care of their physical well-being

- The goal is to:
  - Reduce self-destructive behaviors; including the range, frequency, severity of behaviors.
  - Increase management using alternative healthy behaviors and self-management.
  - Recognizing affect and internal intensity so that it can be managed and contained.
  - To recognize the function or purpose of the behavior to the person.
  - To develop alternative behaviors to serve or be purposeful to the person.
  - To understand the discrepancy between the actual and the desired outcome.
  - To develop a set of values to help create a foundation as a framework for decision making and reference.

- If the patient cannot or will not manage themselves, you can't work beyond where they are capable of managing. The basic outline for therapy is actually very simple, but elegant. This is termed The BASICS (Levitt, 2004).
  - How is what I want to do keeping me safe, secure and physically well?
    - Safety – Internal world management. Managing thoughts, feelings and behaviors.
    - Security – External world management. Managing the people, places and things in ones' life.
    - Physical Well-Being – The functioning of the body and the necessities for health.
  - What are the consequences of my choice (used to manage)?
  - What are all of my alternatives that I could do? And the consequences of each?
  - Is my choice in my best interest (safety, security, physical health; and coherent, congruent, and consistent with what I am trying to achieve?)

How therapy is about age & developmental functioning, and to some extent, parenting
Teaching. It is important to model the skill sets we expect our patients to practice. And, part of doing this also involves teaching the constructs the patient needs to develop. What do we teach? We teach what is important to us. How do we know if something is important? It isn't our words that teach the biggest lesson; it is our ACTIONS that really reflect what is important. Every word, action and behavior by you with another person is a teaching opportunity.

If you parallel process how we teach small children skills to the therapy process, it becomes much clearer and simpler. By this I mean, when we teach children skills, we talk to them very concretely through challenges. We are often encouraging of them; encouraging them to problem solve it, and praising their efforts at trying and at achieving. We verify their comprehension of what we are saying or doing. We show them and then ask them to show us how they do it. It is always a good sign when you observe a child talking to themselves and working their way through mastering something, and then to own that they did it themselves. This mastery is the foundation of age and developmentally appropriate self-regulation. Just because they are verbal, we at times, overestimate their cognitive and emotional levels of capacity. We think that because they are verbal, they understand what we (as adults at a different developmental and life experience level).

Unfortunately, as children become older and more verbal, we, as parents or therapists, tend to change our expectations and move away from this strategy based more on age than actual competencies. As therapists, we assume their expressive language reflects their ability to manage affect laden thoughts, impulses and intensity. When we shift to being less structured and assume that they can manage without regard to the actual evidence, it can be a set up for the person. People, regardless of their age, need structure at the level they are functioning, and to be held accountable for reasonable behavior (within age and developmental parameters).

Goals and Values. It is also important to talk frankly about the goals of treatment. Specifically, it is necessary to discuss whether or not the goal that the person is willing to develop a range of healthy skills to help them manage their safety and well-being. This discussion can clarify their level of preparedness to change and to clarify that they can not be safe and healthy and self-destructive at the same time. While we (the therapist) cannot mandate abstinence from self-destructive behaviors, we can indicate that there are reasonable limits to working with someone who is unwilling to commit to a goal of being safe. Likewise, we can teach parents to set limits and to have reasonable expectations and accountability on their children for age and developmentally appropriate management.

Goals are built on values. Values are important standards or principles we are taught, we learn or choose. When people are not self-regulating they often talk about how random life feels to them, that they don't understand anything. They often talk about how they feel worthless and that life is meaningless. They ask "why should I bother?" This reflects a sense of defeat, often accompanied by anger, resentment and disappointment. While some of this is developmentally appropriate, for our patients with self-destructive patterns, this often drives the emotional fire behind the behavior. When we as therapists avoid the "why" questions, which creates an enormous power struggle, because they will prove to you just how worthless, without value they are, we are avoiding the biggest and most useless conversation ever.

Everyone has value, if they choose to fight you on this, so be it. You have to behave as though you believe they have value and are valuable because they are alive. Period, end of story on that issue. The therapeutic discussion is about how they choose to define themselves and express their self-definition, and is it helpful to them as they create their present and their future. I know this gets a little existential, but it really is kind of rhetorical. The discussion should be about what they hope to create, what outcomes do they want to achieve, and how the current behavior is or isn't working for them. If nothing else, you can discuss whether or not they like the current situation. I am not above pointing out that they are in therapy or in the hospital, and socratically asking what about the current situation they like or is working for them? Many times they won't answer, but that is all right, they heard it. I encourage them to think about it and ask them later what they've been thinking about since I saw them last.

I also acknowledge what I hear them say as being important. I want to clarify what I've heard them say, and ask if they value that concept. Then in further discussion ask them how they practice that in their life, and tie it into the concepts of safety, security and physical well-being. Remember, safety is the management of our thoughts, feelings, reactions and ultimately the choices we make about our behaviors. Security is how we manage our relationships in the external world, the people, places and things we interact with in our lives. Physical well-being is the relationship we have with our own body.

Structure of the Therapeutic Relationship. This stated known expression of expectations and parameters provides the structure that keeps the relationship contained. It gives you the outline for your participation and parameters of your response. When you are structured, and you know the parameters of the relationship, it is much cleaner for both you and the patient. Structure, expectations and accountability help both sides of the relationship.

This relationship is not about emotional attachment and the connectedness of the relationship. The relationship is based on a COMMON GOAL, which is *to develop appropriate age and developmental capacity to self-regulate.* This is often something that therapists need to reconsider: people with self-destructive patterns of managing often do not benefit from emotionally-based connections. Think in regards to healthy attachment formation. Attachment development, in the healthiest sense, comes from the structure, containment and fulfillment of *needs* of the infant during a developmental phase where they cannot provide for themselves. The parent relates to the infants' needs, providing for the *biological needs* and *safety* of the infant. Attachment develops as a result of the continued interaction between the two during this process. The healthiest attachments form based on the biological, developmental and emotional needs of the child by the care-taker, not based on wants, convenience and indulgence.

As a therapist, being aware of the attachment, developmental and maturational needs should be a foundation to organize your approach. The structure serves as a foundation for development of self-regulation. When you refer to the "rules," goals and the values of treatment, you are providing structure for your patient to develop self-regulation. As an example, when you remind the patient about the consequences of their actions, and ask them if their behavior would be consistent with their goals, you are helping remind them of the structure. This actually is also an interaction that can be the opportunity to have a healthy relationship/interaction with another person. Further, when you refer to the agreed upon structure of the relationship, the individual can choose whether or not they want to breech the agreement and incur the consequences of that decision.

Important concepts to keep in mind and to base your interventions on:
1. The goal is to guide/teach the individual self-regulate or self-manage.
2. The goal is to model self-regulation and management in EVERY interaction.
3. Emphasizing behaviors that help move the person towards their desired outcome.
4. Emphasizing problem-solving to tolerate affect and delay of gratification.

5. Containment. We operate on a framework of self-management. It isn't just about the identified patient; *we have to model it too.*
6. The use of the every conversation as an opportunity to provide support and feedback.
7. Every action and word needs to be about self-regulating and containment.
8. Socratic questions are a key to developing self-management. These reflective questions foster the ability to evaluate and think about one's actions and their outcome, and then as a comparison with the desired outcome. That way, you as the therapist, don't provide the "rules of sanity" where you are constantly criticizing or evaluating them, setting up that power struggle.

How do we do this?
1. Goal setting is one way to structure and ground the individual in the focus of all activity.
2. Goal review is the feedback and reality testing to gather data about focus, behavior and accuracy of effort. This process is very concrete and holds people accountable for their stated words. It allows practice for saving face and owning our actions and words.
3. Emphasize reliance on problem-solving strategies, i.e., "what are you willing to try to work through this problem?" Emphasize and encourage when they made the true effort even when the outcome may not have been what they expected. Encourage problem solving for "next time."
4. Emphasizing using healthy people (SECURITY) to ask for feedback and support.
5. Discussing the DATA, true outcomes and known information as opposed to feeling based information.
6. Reminding them about the opportunity to try something new. For example, if the individual is struggling with tolerating affect they can practice management using other activities or "sitting with the feelings," while they "try something new," or goal directed behavior.
7. As a therapist representing both a specific treatment philosophy and a model for self-management, we need to be contained, managing our own stress and feelings appropriately. We have to be willing to practice what we preach, model what we teach, and encourage problem solving when struggling.
8. As a therapist representing both a specific treatment philosophy and a model for self-management, our interventions need to be about the patient attaining self-regulation and management. *Even casual comments and sarcasm can undo your efforts.*
9. We are here because of the patient. But, we are only here as long as the goal is about being healthy and safe. If their goal changes, then the discussion needs to be about their right to leave therapy, and your inability to remain in a therapeutic relationship where they are asking you to condone unsafe or unhealthy behavior. *Note my language; it is deliberate in its choice of words.* I say to patients, when they are choosing to be unhealthy that they have the right not to be in therapy. I also say to them that it is *irresponsible* of me to remain in a therapeutic relationship, where the rule of the relationship is for me to allow someone to be destructive or unsafe. They cannot have *both* a therapeutic relationship and be unsafe and destructive. I state this over and over, and ask them to discuss this openly.

Choice. As a therapist, you need to be prepared to have people opt to leave therapy, and to tell you they aren't willing to be safe and adhere to a therapeutic contract. If they need to be in a higher level of care, then so be it. You may need to face the fact that they can leave treatment *without changing.* If you consider that for many people, the process of change is like that of human development; it goes on for a very long time. There are times that people are not yet ready to change. If you are familiar with the model of motivational interviewing, you will have a greater appreciation for the preparedness for change and the multiple attempts that some people need before observable behaviors happen.

Likewise, you as the therapist can choose to be in and participate in the relationship. You also can set the parameters about how you will remain in the therapeutic relationship. You need to verbalize this and stand by it. Not in a threatening manner, but in a way that models reasonable and responsible management of relationships. I don't negotiate safety, and I don't negotiate the parameters of remaining in a relationship where the individual chooses to be unhealthy, dishonest and unwilling to follow the agreed upon parameters.

Translating into "Real Life" Experience

Some think the person in therapy is "the problem." They may not understand that we are social creatures, and our family is the first experience we have with the world. That means, our family is where we learn about how to manage ourselves and our relationships with other people. These other people have different obligations, experiences, responsibilities and privileges than we might have. So teaching people about being a part of a *unit* or place for our first social learning is absolutely important. However, people don't often understand how the system they are in/were raised in may have influenced them in their development.

Many times families say they want their "kids to be kids," because life will be hard enough later. What they don't recognize is that part of being a kid is learning about how to live in the world. The skills and competencies they develop in their childhood are the foundation for what they take into their adulthood. Without the years of reasonable practicing and developing skills, when they leave their childhood home, they have no skills to manage.

What skills are learned? Being totally practical at first, let's look at what we learn as a child that can help us manage our own household. This can include skills for managing:
- A household. This includes skills for cooking, cleaning, laundry, money management, paying bills, scheduling activities, and the importance meal and family activities.
- Relationships with others and with self.
- Rules for life.

Now, take it to the next level. This is a developmental shift. Just like how development happens in stages in ages, emotional, language and maturation shifts occur too.
- Self-care. This involves hygiene, cleanliness, dental/physical/eye care, healthy routines for sleep, physical activities, and healthy nutrition.

- Relationships. These skills include recognizing healthy/unhealthy relationships, negotiating and conflict resolution, getting needs met, respecting boundaries and limits.
- Goals, Expectations and Achievement. This involves having an understanding of what they are working towards, and that their efforts are helpful in attaining what they set out to get. This is the "IF I...THEN..." in action.

In therapy, we talk with our patients about their goals and expectations, and how we are going to help there be accountability for their actions. Talking with families about *reasonable* expectations and accountability is a critical first step in treatment too. Asking a family what their values are and how they demonstrate it in their daily lives is a critical foundation issue for families. Often the answer I hear is that they are "too busy" or that they never thought about it. This is like taking off on a sailboat into open water without knowing how to sail, where you are going, or what you need and then being surprised and angry when they get lost, take on water or get into trouble when the sea gets rough. Likewise, they don't often understand how they are part of the crew of the darn boat!

Further, as children become older and more verbal, we also provide less and less positive encouragement, and more negative feedback, especially if their behavior displeases or inconveniences us. As therapists, it is neither helpful to them to be overly praising or to be punitive. Our emotional tone is *neutral*, looking at the evidence or data of the situation. Our role is to be a teacher of skills and to allow them to think their way through alternatives. Further, it is helpful to ask them if they desire/prefer the outcome of their choices. This is the "IF ....., THEN...." sequence. Working through this and allowing them to see the cause-effect of their challenges is part of helping them developmentally move to become more self-regulating and self-efficacious.

As the child gains more verbal ability, our structure changes and we begin to reassess the structure, responsibilities and privileges they have available to them. However, when privileges and rewards are given without attachment to appropriate self-management, actual skill level and self-management capacities, it may be a set up for them. An example would be when you have a 16-year-old who is failing at school, often claims to be suicidal, is engaging in self-destructive and risky behaviors like promiscuous sex and substance abuse, and you give them the car keys and tell them they were "good today" and tell them they can have the car; and you are tired of fighting with them, so you give them "their" cell phone and don't monitor their computer usage. In this example, the behaviors, expectations and privileges are not connected to age and developmentally appropriate functioning. So they don't connect increased appropriate responsibility and self-management to increased freedoms and privileges.

The parents may be quick at restricting them from their cell phones, computers, privileges, etc., but this is at the cost of the lesson. The lesson *should be* that privileges are earned as a result of first and foremost, consistent demonstration that the child is able to keep themselves safe and healthy. The other critical concept here is that these kids often have too much freedom and privilege and they need structure, clearly stated rules and expectations and to be held accountable BEFORE they are given the material privileges and privileges they can't emotionally handle. Consequently, many kids become very entitled, "I deserve it," or "how dare you," without it being connected to the concept of investment in earning it through demonstrating reasonably consistent self-management and investment in the family. This is a critical concept for families to address in therapy.

Often the family wants to be "good" or "kind" at the expense of teaching a child a lesson in self-regulation and reasonable expectations for appropriate behavior. Additionally, the person never develops the skills to manage frustration and delay gratification. Since the kid has not had the opportunity to develop self-reliance and investment in earning anything, they become angry when they have any demands placed on them. This pattern denies the person the opportunity to go through normal healthy developmental maturation. Self-destructive behavior keeps the person at an immature and arrested developmental stage, where they can't delay gratification, tolerate frustration and manage emotions and negotiate healthy relationships.

One example of this is the early sexualization of our children when they are not emotionally mature enough to handle social relationships well and are still greatly struggling with self-definition. This is a typical developmental stage struggle in healthy adolescent development. However for these kids, they aren't able to manage or tolerate relationships, with themselves or with others in healthy manners. Their angst is handled through either acting out or acting in. Self-destructive behaviors either increase or decrease the internal experience, or serve to communicate or connect with another person (Nock & Kessler, 2006). In the case of self-destructive behaviors though, there is a correlation with a section of this group who has a history of abuse. That question should always be asked. That being said, the early sexualization of these children, when they are unable to have healthy relationships with their own "self" and their own body, doesn't often bode well. These children/teens connect with people who are typically not healthy or managing well either. And, parents often condone this, and put their child on the pill or provide condoms (which is responsible), but the issue is, they don't step in and dialogue repeatedly about family values, self-respect and expectations. This is a healthier alternative than telling a kid who can't self-regulate that they can dress sexually provocatively or otherwise provocatively and can be sexually active. This turns the interaction into one about self-respect, dignity, and self-definition.

Our conversations with our children are often interactions where it appears they have most of the language skills, but not much in the way of true life experience and understanding of concepts is limited to their age and life experience. Adolescent brains are wired to be responsive with emotion before logic. Consequently, they respond intensely and can quickly disintegrate into an intensely emotional situation. Parents often either respond emotionally and loudly back, and then there are two sources of escalation fighting for power. Other times parents back down, because they are defeated or because they don't want conflict. This denies the child/teen the opportunity to learn how to appropriately resolve conflict and tolerate disappointment, frustration and authority. Often the consequences don't match the behavior and aren't about the family structure and expectations. The "rewards" and "privileges" are actually quite often more about convenience and entitlement. As therapists, it is our job to make the logical connections between actions and outcomes, responsibilities and privileges.

In working with families, especially with parents, it is important to orient them to *what they want in their family*. This is the foundation providing the structure and guidance. Often basic calibration in terms of establishing reasonable limits, expectations, accountability and responsibility/privileges is exactly what these patients need and crave. They can't develop self-regulation well if the family is not regulated. Working on some of the basic family values and creating a family unit is one way to begin this work. Discussing consistent anchoring of these concepts into practice is an important conversation to have. It is important to consider that everyone living in the home should be considered part of the system, no one is exempt.

I try to be direct about this, although attempt to be mindful of their level of ability and investment in this process. Some families are not willing or ability to provide what patients need. In that case, you may have to teach your patient about limitations of people we love, and help them grieve some losses they experience. Teaching someone about limitations involves recognizing disappointments, loss of dreams and hopes for a family.

Intervention involves the same things but on a level involving the family. We say the same things to families/parents about their actions and choices and their desired outcomes that we say about the kid/teen. We remind them how important they are to the recovery process. Some families will allow the therapists input, others won't or can't.

Last thoughts on HOW TO do therapy with someone who self-injures
There is little "magic" about therapy with individuals who self-injure. You must be certain you understand your approach and conceptualization, and be structured in your approach. Think your way through the process. Structure and contain, then process efforts at managing. Encourage tolerance of affect, delay of gratification, impulse control and learning from experience. Develop and foster expressive language skills and teach listening and understanding while minimizing affective and impulsive reactions.

Think developmentally. It is important to look at the emotional and developmental stage of functioning and the discrepancy with actual age and place in life. You have to model the behavior you want the patient to develop. Being consistent with expectations, and holding them accountable is critical. Understanding that privileges are earned and need to be contingent upon age and developmental appropriate is important to healthy development. Understanding that the behavior is purposeful and how it is purposeful are the important starting points for interventions. The rest builds from there towards a goal of creating a lifestyle that is based on healthy self-management.

Saying the same thing over and over is part of the teaching process. We call this consistency. It builds predictability and constancy into the structure. This becomes part of self-regulating.

Anchoring choices to outcomes is important. Being consistent with expectations, accountability and being based in age and developmental appropriateness is very important part of the learning process. Fostering hope, being compassionate to the struggle, while believing they are capable of making positive choices and healthy management is the foundation of healthy functioning and self-regulation.

If we use more Socratic questions, cueing evaluation of their own thinking and behaviors, we offer them the opportunity to create the connection between choices and outcomes. Secondly, they can create options and alternatives anchored in our stated expectations, values and desired outcomes/goals. We don't take the position then of judging them. However, it is important that we be willing to provide commentary about whether or not things are reasonable or not, appropriate or not, healthy or not. Keep in mind that they own the consequences of their actions; we can provide some structure in evaluating this outcome.

We, as parents and as therapists, often TALK TOO MUCH. We talk until we think/feel they understand us. What happens is that they stop listening, generally because they are so flooded with affect and internal intensity. This provokes some of the shutting down, and some of the "urge" to injure to drive down internal intensity. Remember, it is pretty typical of adolescents to experience when they are being talked to and they are being challenged, to describe this as "being yelled at" and they don't listen. At this point the power struggle to save face and "win" the battle becomes the goal. Be creative, use physical activities, such as relaxation, breathing and stretching. Use art, color, and collages with mixed media. Use metaphors, fables and mantras. Providing alternatives augment the verbal message and makes the process of learning more fun and experiential.

Introduction to the Activities: Building the Foundation

Framework for Recovery: Contract with Myself

Daily Focus Activities
Morning Meditation
Evening Daily Acknowledgement
Core Exercise A: Getting Grounded
Core Exercise B: Creating Safety
Core Exercise C: Free Journaling Blitz Review of the Day

The Journal Assignments

Note the use of sayings and quotes. There are also cues for breathing and centering yourself. The mind-body connection is an important part of creating something new. Your mind and body are connected. What you say to yourself changes your body. It is a cycle. When you slow your mind and connect with your body, you create an opportunity for health and hope for the future.

Because if you've found meaning in your life, you don't want to go back. You want to go forward.... It's not to late to... ask yourself if you really are the person you want to be, and if not, who you do want to be. Morrie Schwartz

---

Introduction to the Activities: Building the Foundation

As a start, complete the _Contract with Myself._ It is the focus of your move towards being healthy and creating a new present. It is a commitment to yourself and your future as you contract with yourself to work towards being healthy and safe. You can do this contract over and over and over. Be realistic about making little changes, one at a time. These little changes build into new habits and direction

The second set of activities is the _Daily Focus Activities._ Your day can start with a Meditation and end with the Daily Acknowledgement.
- These include the _Morning Meditation_ designed to focus your attention on a specific recovery or health aspect for the day.
- The _Evening Daily Acknowledgement_ is a journal entry made at the end of the day to review what you worked on during the day.

The _Core Exercises_ include a set of foundation exercises that can be done repeatedly.
- The Core Exercises A, B, & C emphasize Creating Purpose, Grounding and Safety. These include _Free_ and _Focused_ journaling exercises.
  - Core Exercise A involves creating purpose and involves practicing being grounded and connected through all five senses.
  - Core Exercise B involves awareness and creation of internal safety (managing our reactions, thoughts, feelings and behaviors in a mindful and purposeful manner).
  - Core Exercise C is an opportunity to review the activities of the day and the daily focus towards your goals. It also contains you, so you don't get overwhelmed by your feelings and reactions. Try to be mindful and use you breathing as you fill in the space given. You can use words, symbols, colors, or whatever you'd like (as long as it is healthy).
- _You can work on any or all of the Core Exercises at any time you need to refocus._

The Journal Assignments includes writing exercises and assignments. Each has a specific focus, lesson and written activity.
- Work one page at a time. Commit a specific amount of time to start and when to finish writing. It is recommended to allot between 15 – 30 minutes daily.
- Think about what you write. This is the foundation of mindfulness. It is purposeful; how can you practice what you've written?
- Look for opportunities to think differently about something you do the same over and over.
- Commit to a period of time where you look for opportunities to try something new and practice what you wrote.
- Commit to your journaling in brief amounts several times a day, think of it as a commitment to your health.
- Be mindful of your choices, reactions, behaviors and attitudes.

"If you don't know where you are going, how will you know when you've gotten there?"

Note: Throughout this journal, you will see sayings, statements and quotes, like above and below. Take a moment to think about the saying. Breathe deeply and become connected to your mind and body. Think about it throughout the day. Use it to help you focus on one specific idea as a guiding light. If it really touches you, write it on a note card and keep it with you. Use it as a healthy and soothing statement you repeat when you are anxious or afraid. Use it when you have an important choice or decision to make. Use it to keep yourself grounded and focused. ***Remember what you think creates your reality!*** *Perception is colored by your attitude and belief system. Changing your thinking, means literally thinking about the world differently!*

The **Contract with Myself** is a journaling exercise as a beginning to your recovery process. This Contract is to help you clarify what you are working on and will be focused in your recovery. The Contract helps provide the framework for setting your goals, being focused and making healthy decisions in your life. You may want to re-evaluate your goals from time to time. This assignment will serve as your map and reference as you work towards being healthy.

Suggestions for Goals:
- Happiness is a great destination, but not a great goal. Happiness, contentment and all those positive feeling states, and are by-products of the way you live your life.
- Set realistic and reasonable goals that you can tell easily if you've worked towards them.
- Remember feelings aren't reality (Feelings aren't facts, they tell you when something important is going on, they are CUES to pay attention). Look for DATA, which is behavior based.
- Keep in mind that you may not FEEL like being healthy, but you can still chose what you do.
- Ideas to consider:
    - Keep myself safe when feeling destructive
    - Make a list of healthy/safe choices
    - Use the list of healthy/safe choices
    - Pay attention to when I get upset and start feeling like I want to hurt myself
    - Try something healthy
    - Set healthy boundaries on my friends who let me be destructive
    - Set limits on phone calls with my mom – when I get angry I can end the call
    - Use words not actions to say when I'm upset
    - Say how I feel about things
    - Feelings are not facts
    - Words and actions have consequences, choose wisely

Something to think about…………..

1. Time teaches slowly, often at the expense of mistakes. It is an opportunity to learn.
2. Be kind to yourself when you don't get the results you want. It is an opportunity to practice compassion and self-respect while creating hope.
3. Keep working towards the goals you set. Be consistent.
4. Your feelings don't determine whether you have succeeded or not. Your actions and outcomes do.
5. Behavior serves a purpose, but sometimes the purpose isn't helpful. It is an opportunity to try something new and create a new purpose.
6. Your behavior and choices show your true motivation. This is an opportunity to be honest with yourself and to match your intentions and your actions (live congruently). Be mindful.
7. You are responsible for the choices you make.
8. You are not responsible for the choices other people make.
9. You are responsible for your words and actions.
10. You are not responsible for the words and actions of others.
11. You are responsible for your feelings and how you manage your feelings.
12. You are not responsible for other peoples' feelings and what they do with them.
13. You are responsible for what you contribute to relationships.
14. "Suicidal" is not a feeling, when people say this they often mean they are overwhelmed and feel almost unable to manage. Take these words seriously; be precise about what you mean. Are you overwhelmed, or are you truly suicidal?

In the long run, we shape our lives, and we shape ourselves. The process never ends until we die. And the choices we make are ultimately our own responsibility. Eleanor Roosevelt

---

Worksheet for the Contract with Myself

Define your goals in terms of behaviors you can see and know when and how you are doing them.

1. Set a destination. What is something you want to accomplish?

Without goals, and plans to reach them, you are like a ship that has set sail with no destination. Fitzhugh Dodson

2. What is something that is necessary for you to do to reach that goal?

Start by doing what's necessary, then what's possible, and suddenly you are doing the impossible. Francis of Assisi

3. What are you willing to believe about yourself to make this happen?

To accomplish great things, we must not only act, but also dream, not only plan, but also believe.
Anatole France

4. Why change now? If you could picture your change, imagine it.

If not us, who? If not now, when? John F. Kennedy

_____

5. What is something I am able to do or something I am that can help me?

They are able because they think they are able. Virgil

_____

6. What is something that I am willing to do to help myself?

We all have ability. The difference is how we use it. Stevie Wonder

_____

Framework for Recovery: Contract with Myself

Purpose:
- Clarify what I am working towards *for this time in my life*.
- Clarify what I am willing and not willing to do to work towards those goals.

I am willing to work on certain things because my life situation is not what I wanted or needed it to be.

What I want:	Why I want/need to change:	What am I willing to do differently?	What will I have to give up?

My contract with myself:
I agree to work towards making changes in my life. *For this time between* _____ *and* _____, I am willing to focus on change and I my goal for my:

1. SAFETY *or my internal world of thoughts, feelings & reactions*:

2. SECURITY *or the way I manage relationships with the people, places & things in my world:*

3. PHYSICAL WELL- BEING *or the way I attend to the needs of my body where I reside and from where I interact with the world.*

4. Values *I will focus on and be mindful of during this time:*

I will:
- Be mindful of the values I want to build into my life.
- Work on these goals honestly.
- Ask for help from healthy resources when I need them.
- Be focused on, mindful and aware of my goals.
- Know my goals, and review them daily. If I get lost, I will come back to my goals.
- Ask for support and help from healthy people.
- Treat myself with dignity, compassion and respect.

I agree to stay alive and not engage in dangerous behaviors. I agree to ask for help before I act on impulse. I agree to look for and use healthy behaviors to replace self-destructive patterns.

Review and/or repeat this activity as many times as is necessary as you work.

Signed:_____ Date:_____

One can choose to go back toward safety or forward toward growth. Growth must be chosen again and again; fear must be overcome again and again. Abraham Maslow

The journaling activity has several purposes:
1. To express your thoughts and feelings.
2. To increase your awareness of how you see and think about your world.
3. To increase your awareness of how you respond to your thoughts and perceptions.
4. To focus your awareness own yourself and your treatment, and to integrate your goals for recovery with your own reflections, perceptions and daily living.
5. To identify opportunities to identify and to interrupt patterns, and create new options and alternatives to create a new future.

Daily Focus Activities

1. Every morning begin with the **Morning Meditation** journal entry.
   The goal of this exercise is to help identify the *focus* of your attention throughout the day. Setting goals and being mindful of how they become integrated into your daily recovery is an important practice in developing new patterns of thinking and behaving.
2. In the evening, complete **Evening Daily Acknowledgement** journal entry.
   This activity is to review what you have worked on during the day.
3. The **Core Activities** include the **Focused** and **Free** journaling exercises.
   * These activities are the daily assignments to work on related to your recovery activities. They help to your work towards your goals become patterns of living and staying safe. *You can work on any or all of the Core Exercises at any time you need to refocus.*
4. Some days will have specific exercises assigned or of your own choosing to focus yourself.

You might want to complete these exercises in your notebook, as you might want to have the structure available to you to rework the exercises throughout your recovery process.

Note about Goals:

1. Focus on writing about behaviors or thoughts you can identify.
   Today my goal is to use my deep breathing when I notice I am tense.
   When I have a negative thought, I will reframe it so that it is more positive.
2. Focus on goals written in positive terms you can be mindful of during the day.
   I will use my coping skills instead of self-injury instead of "I won't hurt myself."
3. Keep your eye on the big picture, your daily goals show a part of the bigger goal.
   Because I want to learn to keep myself safe, today I will use my positive coping list if I feel like hurting myself. I see myself making good choices. (See it, picture it, draw it).
4. To help build success into your recovery, goals should be:
   a. Realistic   They are something that are real
   b. Reasonable   They are something that are possible
   c. Attainable   They are something that you can reach
   d. Meaningful   They have value to you
   e. Healthy   They keep you Safe, Secure, and Physically Well
   f. Offer an opportunity to learn something new!

Think about what you want to work on in recovery. Practice writing these are goals here:

Whatever you are, be a good one. Abraham Lincoln

Morning Meditation Format

My overall focus in recovery *for today* is:

Related to my *SAFETY* (internal processes leading my thinking, feeling and behaviors), my goal:

Related to my *SECURITY* (external world, relationships with people, places and things in my life), my goal:

Related to my *PHYSICAL WELL-BEING*, my goal:

I will work on recognizing patterns and how they affect my life:
Thinking patterns (Example: *I will recognize negative thinking*):

Behaving patterns (Example: *I will focus on my breathing*):

Feeling/reaction patterns (Example: *I will tolerate my feelings without acting*):

To practice being mindful, my motto (focus) for today is:

What lies behind us and what lies before us are tiny matters compared to what lies within us. Ralph Waldo Emerson

Today, I worked on a number of things, and I know this because I:

I kept my BASICS in mind and in practice, in the following ways:
Safety:
Security:
Physical Well-Being:

Ten things/people/thoughts, I am grateful for today (more if I need to):

Today, I think I began to understand:

Although I am still struggling with:

Tomorrow, I will work on:

And ask for help with:

I'm willing to give myself credit for…

My closing thought for myself tonight is:

IT IS BETTER TO LIGHT A CANDLE THAN TO CURSE THE DARKNESS.
MOTTO OF THE CHRISTOPHER SOCIETY

What light did you bring into your own life today to make it better?

Getting Grounded– Foundation of Being Connected and Creating Safety.

Get grounded into the present using the five senses in the moment.

- Use your senses and your breathing to change your connection with the present. Orient and ground yourself with the moment, and relax your body. Your body responds to information you give it. Teach your body to be present and work with your mind as you concentrate and focus. Calm you body with the messages you say to it. What you say to yourself sets the tone to how your body will respond and react.
- You may want to use a scented lotion for warmth and scent, or mints for taste, etc.
- Pay attention to your world, look around and experience it in the moment.
- See yourself standing firmly on the ground, stretching to the sky, being connected to the world.
  a. At this moment, what do I see? (List 3-5) What is surrounding me?
      Breathe slowly & deeply. Count to 4. Listen to your breath.
  b. At this moment, what do I hear? (List 3-5)
      Breathe slowly & deeply. Count to 4. Calmly listen to your world.
  c. At this moment, what do I taste? (List 3-5)
      Breathe slowly & deeply. Count to 4.
  d. At this moment, what do I smell? (List 3-5)
      Breathe slowly & deeply. Count to 4.
  e. At this moment, on a scale of 1 to 10 how tense do I feel? (List 3-5)
      Breathe slowly & deeply. Count to 4.
  f. As you breathe, in slowly & evenly, picture your body becoming calmer, more aware of the world around you. Create a picture in your mind, see colors, see a symbol of change, picture yourself being calm

Points to Wonder

1. What was I working towards today? What goals did I focus on?
2. What did I do to stay focused and mindful on them today?
3. What was helpful? What wasn't? What seems to work best for me?
4. What did I learn today?
5. What was most useful to me today?
6. How did I manage to stay focused on what was in my best interest?
7. What did I respond to today that was not positive or helpful to me? Was I aware of them at the time? How did I react?
8. What did I do to manage in a healthy manner?
9. What positive things can I say to myself about my efforts today?
10. In what way(s) am I creating purpose in my life? Purpose that is meaningful, constructive, that is in my best interest, and keeps me safe, secure & physically well

---

Sow a thought, and you reap an act;
Sow an act, and you reap a habit;
Sow a habit, and you reap a character;
Sow a character, and you reap a destiny. Samuel Smiles

Being grounded and connected to the world in the present allows you to participate actively in your world. It helps you be connected and present. It helps your brain tell if there are real threats or ghosts of old ones, or false alarms. When your brain and body are connected and giving each other information about the present moment, you may find you are less anxious, scared and impulsive.

SAFETY: Is an internal process that puts into order how we manage our reactions, thoughts, feelings and behaviors into mindful and purposeful behavior. It governs our internal reality and colors how we interact with our external world.

Breathe and practice being grounded and connected to the world around you (5 things).

What makes it difficult for you to be grounded and connected?

Do you have specific situations, circumstances or events that can cause you to lose your groundedness? Are they predictable?

What thoughts are in your head while you attend to these things?

Are they helpful or distracting?

What are five things you can do daily to help you be grounded?

Practice being grounded and focused now. What is different than when you started this exercise?

Get grounded into the present using the five senses. As you work through each sense, take time to pay attention to your breathing. Key your eyes open. Practice slow, rhythmic breathing as you go through this exercise below. Try to practice five-ten of each below:

> *a. At this moment, what do I see? What is surrounding you?*
> *b. At this moment, what do I hear?*
> *c. At this moment, what do I taste?*
> *d. At this moment, what do I smell?*
> *e. At this moment, what do I feel?*
> *f. Breathe slowly and picture yourself being calm and connected.*

Do you notice a change in your level of awareness or body tension?
On a scale from 1 – 10, monitor your state of tension before and after the exercises.

Describe where your body holds its tension or feelings.

Practice this three times during your day.

I am creating myself everyday, I am in process of living my life,
Each day is a brand new opportunity that I have some say in, that I can impact.
I can't change the past, however, what can I create now?

Free-journaling: Brief Blitzes!

Limit your free journaling time to *5 to 10* minutes daily or just in the space below. Just write about your feelings and reactions to people and events that happened during the day today while you were working on your goals.

Stay focused *on the day, not the past or any other time*. Describe the day in as much detail as you need to make your point. Pay attention to your memories of your five senses during these events. Pay attention to what you wrote. Why is it important? Write for five minutes. *Then stop*.

What is important to recall about the day?

What positive self-statement can you use to encourage yourself about your work today?

It's not what you have, it's what you do with what you have

The JOURNAL
Journaling Exercises & Assignments

Exercise 1: Self-Talk or "A Note About Myself"

It's not what you look at that matters, it's what you see. Henry David Thoreau

Write a letter to yourself about:
- What do you want to change in your life? What isn't working anymore?
- Why do you want to change now?
- How your self-destructive behavior helps you, what it costs you.
- What are you willing to do differently? What aren't you willing to do?

Exercise 1: Self-Talk or "A Note about Myself" continued

About me, I was born on _____ at _____.

I was raised to believe _____.

My family_____.

The people I was raised with/by include:

As a child, I was described as_____.

I loved_____.

For fun, we would_____.

My favorite_____.

My mother_____.

She taught me_____.

In her life my mother believed that (list at least three):

My father_____.

He taught me_____.

In his life my father believed that (list at least three):

Looking at what I learned from watching my parents relationship with each other, I learned:

In my family, we_____.

I could never_____.

We_____.

I tried to be like my mother_____.

I tried to be like my father_____.

One rule I broke was_____.

I got in trouble_____.

I was afraid to_____.

I was afraid of_____.

Write about some of the rules you grew up with:

A funny story about me:

In my family, I learned:

We could talk about_____.

But not about_____.

Getting in trouble meant_____.

We celebrated_____.

What was important to my family_____.

What was important to me_____.

What my family wanted for me was:

I always wanted to_____.

I looked forward to _____.

My friends_____.

Once we:

From my friends, I learned_____.

I was pretty good at_____.

I wished I_____.

I dreamed about_____.

I hated_____.

I disliked_____.

I didn't care about_____.

I liked_____.

I loved_____.

I felt loved when_____.

What five important things I learned about life from growing up in my family:

What five important ways I am different than my family:

List 10 things that are important to you (values, beliefs, memories, hopes, dreams):

Exercise 2: What I Want You to Know About Me

A leader has two important characteristics; first, he is going somewhere; second, he is able to persuade other people to go with him. Robespierre

Pick someone you want to tell about you. Tell them the important things about you and your self-destructive behaviors. It may be helpful to write this to help your therapist get to know you.

- What do you want to change in your life? What isn't working anymore?
- Why do you want to change now?
- How your self-destructive behavior helps you, what it costs you.
- What are you willing to do differently? What aren't you willing to do?

Was I honest?

Exercise 3: Understanding the Choices I Make

It takes more courage to reveal insecurities than to hide them,
more strength to relate to people than to dominate them,
more "manhood" to abide by thought-out principles rather than blind reflex.
Alex Karras

It is important to understand that you make choices about your behaviors. Self-destructive behaviors help you manage. This is something that is difficult for many people to understand.

What are behaviors you use to help you stay alive and manage your feelings?

How are these behaviors helpful to you?

What kind of problems do you get into because of your self-destructive behaviors?

Exercise 4: Who I Want to Become

Throughout the centuries there were men who took first steps down new roads armed with nothing but their own vision. Ayn Rand

It helps to have an idea of what you want to move towards as you grow through your life. Before you start, take an inventory of those qualities you would like to build upon or develop. Who do you want to become? I want to be someone who has/is:

For example, Peaceful, mindfulness, hope, friends, sobriety, health

For each of these, what do you think will be helpful to you to practice so you can become more like that?

For example: Peace: Practice grounding when I am upset

Write a positive statement for yourself to help keep you focused on who you are becoming:

Am I willing to consider this might be true?

Exercise 5: Taking My Inventory

To accomplish great things, we must not only act, but also dream, not only plan, but also believe. Anatole France

You are a complex and rich person, with many qualities and abilities that you may not give yourself credit for having. By being alive, you have value, you are worthwhile and valuable. How you define yourself will be your foundation for your recovery and growth. If you are working on this, and being honest with yourself, then you also need to be willing to acknowledge that you have skills, strengths and value. These can be built with mindful awareness and choice of action.

Are there specific things about how you want to change? For example, if you tend to be very emotional, perhaps you want to be less emotional and more thoughtful before you act.

What you are willing to change	How you think you could do that

Identify some ways you could change your thoughts, reactions (feelings) and behaviors.

Instead of:	I could practice:

Look for opportunities to practice changing your thoughts, reactions and feelings. Write about them in your evening journal!

Exercise 6: Mastering My Fear of Letting Go of Self-Destructive Behaviors

Start by doing what's necessary, then what's possible, and suddenly you are doing the impossible. Francis of Assisi

It is hard to give up something that has helped you, even if it has cost you in some ways. If you've used self-destructive behaviors to cope and manage your life, you may have stopped allowing yourself to feel certain feelings. You may also believe that you can't have a life without using self-destructive behaviors to manage your life.

One of the first steps is imaging your life without self-destructive behaviors. What do you think will your life would be like without self-destructive behaviors? Use words, pictures, or symbols.

If you were willing to not use self-destructive behaviors, what do you think would be the hardest part for you?

What are some other ways you could do to help you manage your thoughts and feelings? List them.

Are you willing to try any of these other ways?

Exercise 7: Talking to Myself

They are able because they think they are able. Virgil

We talk to ourselves all the time. Sometimes we are not even aware of what we say and how it affects us. Our internal conversations help us plan, problem-solve, rehearse, remember or resolve things. Sometimes these conversations reinforce our patterns, beliefs and attitudes. What you say to yourself have an effect on your belief system, attitudes, physiology and actions. This may or may not be helpful.

Being mindful of our self-talk and its effect on us is an important part of our recovery process.
What are some self-statements that you make that are NOT helpful?

How could re-write these self-statement s to be more encouraging or helpful to you?

Write at least eight encouraging or positive self-statements that you can say to yourself. When can you practice using them?

Positive Self-Statement	When I can use this.....

Write these positive reframes on note cards for you to keep in your folder to use if you need encouragement.

Practice these and use your deep breathing. Say them slowly, focus and breathe.

Exercise 8: Clustering Important Ideas around "MY BEST INTERESTS"

About my **SAFETY** what do I have to keep in mind?

Safety: the internal processes (inside our minds and body) that manages thoughts, feelings and behaviors. It is the way we think and manage ourselves. That is why breathing, paying attention and having our minds and bodies connected is so important.

• The purpose for taking care of my Safety is:

This means managing my thoughts, my feelings and behaviors, and making healthy choices, staying grounding, learning from my life. This means being responsible for myself and my health.

• Why do I want to change my self-destructive thinking, feelings, attitude or behavior? Is it for me or someone else? How do I think my life will be different?

• Do I like the way things are right now? This means thinking about the consequences (outcomes) of my actions or behaviors? Explain:

    For example, do you like that people don't trust you that you aren't going to hurt yourself?

About my **SECURITY**, I have to keep what things in mind every day?

Security: the external processes (our interactions with the outside world) that govern the choices about the people, places and things in your life. This is the way we manage our relationships with our world and others.

- Taking care of my security means making healthy choices about where I go, who I am with, and what I choose to do. The purpose for taking care of my Security is:

- What gets in the way of taking care of my Security?

- How do I want to change my patterns of having self-destructive people, places and things in my life?

- In order to create security, what do I have to consider changing?

For my **PHYSICAL WELL-BEING**, what do I have to keep in mind every day?

   Physical Well-Being: ways of practicing self-care and health. This is the relationship you have with your body, yourself and your commitment to taking care of yourself.

- The purpose for taking care of my Physical Well-Being is:

- What is the biggest problem about taking care of my health and my body?

- Why do I want to change my self-destructive behaviors that affect my body?

- What do I have to be *willing* to change even if I don't *want* to change?

What does it mean to take make decisions *in my best interest?* What do I need to change?

Exercise 9: Recognizing Patterns

My **THINKING** becomes destructive when:

When I am self-destructive, am I more in the present or past? How so? How does that happen?

My **BEHAVIOR** becomes destructive when:

Being self-destructive "helps" me to:

But…..What I am really doing is:

Some of the negative outcomes of being self-destructive are:

Other ways to feel in control might be to:

What do I have to be willing to do or try in order to feel like I have control or manage pain that is not self-destructive?

He who would learn to fly one day must first learn to stand and walk and run and climb and dance; one cannot fly into flying. Friedrich Wilhelm Nietzsche

Exercise 10: Masks

We get used to wearing masks; pretending to think, feel or believe things that we really don't. There are consequences or costs to living with this pattern. Our outward appearances might not match what is really under the surface are our real thought, feelings and beliefs. We call this *incongruence*.

We struggle with the aftermath, the emotional intensity that builds and builds. There are ways to calm this turmoil, but how mindful are we about our choices? What are the other choices?

I wear masks or act differently than I honestly think or feel when (list at least 3):

When I act differently from how I honestly want to, I end up feeling, thinking or believing:

Right now inside, my feelings are:

What are some other ways safer ways I could try to manage the differences between my feelings, my actions and honest thoughts and feelings?

How often do I respond or react honestly? When is it healthy to do this? When is it not healthy?

Slowly breathe in and out, as you become calm and centered, picture yourself without your masks.

You can't depend on your eyes when your imagination is out of focus. **Mark Twain**

I don't know the key to success, but the key to failure is trying to please everybody. Bill Cosby

---

Recognize where you let people stand in relation to you. Not everyone *deserves* to be close to you or be allowed access to your resources, favors, friendship, secrets or emotions. How close do you allow people to be? Do you allow people closer than they deserve? Where are you willing to move them away from you emotionally? What do you need to do internally to manage these moves? Our boundaries are based on who we are dealing with, what we feel about them, the safety of the relationship, the health or demands of the situation, etc. *You have choices about your own safety and limits.* You have the responsibility and right to manage yourself in these relationships in keeping yourself safe and secure.

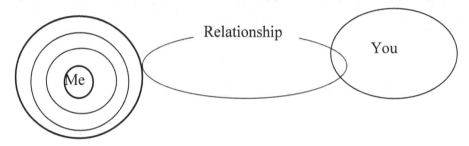

Here is an example of a relationship where I (me) don't let you get too close with me. This might be where I am polite, civil, but don't share anything personal with you. I also would listen to what you have to say, but not react too personally. If you were closer, my behavior and reactions might be different. As the rings go out, the person isn't as close and the relationship may not be that personal or intimate.

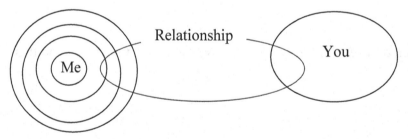

Here is an example of what a friendship might look like. Both people are in the relationship, and here, on the second ring, the rules change a bit. More sharing and closeness, trust and caring happen.

Think about yourself and your rings. What are the rules for each ring?

Think about the people in your life, draw in those rings.

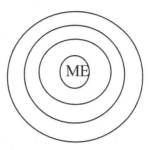

Using **the initials of people in your life,** mark healthy people and relationships you have in your life, and how close they are to you on the intimacy circles.

Map out, using **"X",** unhealthy people and relationships you have in your life, and how close they are to you on the intimacy circles.

Who are safe people? What makes them safe? *How do you know they are safe*?

How close do you let them in and why?

At which ring is TRUST EARNED?

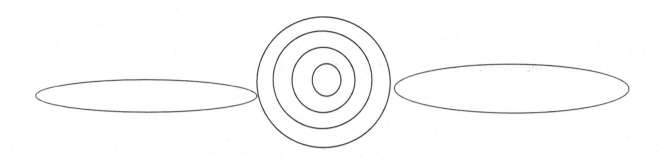

Who are people in my life that I should have more distance from, that you should move further out from how "close" should you let them be emotionally?

What would happen or are you afraid of if you set limits, emotionally distance myself or say "no" to others:

People/Situations where you feel take advantage of you:

What are the definitions of each ring? Think of the rules or definitions of each so you can be clear on closest friend/person all the way out to acquaintance and stranger.

I can state my mind, set my limits, and take care of myself.
I don't have to give my power and self-respect away.

Exercise 12: Values & Personal Rules

Values and goals, like a beacon, help us to decide what direction we move. They help us to make decisions when we are uncertain. They are the foundations of our lives.

Today I am the author of my life. I chose what matters.
Some values from childhood I keep, others I alter.
My values and beliefs are evident in the choices I make and the way I behave.

Some rules are *not* helpful to keep. They might impact your health or cause consequences in your life that you don't like. In what ways might your beliefs negatively impact your BASICS or your best interests? *List at least five beliefs you hold onto that work against your goals and BASICS.*

1.

2.

3.

4.

5.

Write *10 values* you feel are important for you to live by, that help you maintain your BASICS and best interests? How do these values do that for you?

Using some or all of the 10 values you selected, rewrite those unhealthy rules.

Exercise 13: Refocus & Review ~ What do I want?

Destiny is no matter of chance. It is a matter of choice: It is not a thing to be waited for; it is a thing to be achieved. William Jennings Bryan
The tragedy of life doesn't lie in not reaching your goal. The tragedy lays in have no goal to reach. Benjamin Mays

It helps to review your position in your recovery from time to time. You may have shifted and not even been aware. Take some time to review your efforts and allow for change and accomplishments.

What were the reasons that you came into treatment?

What is one goal to focus on right now?

Why is that goal important to me?

What do I do to stay focused on and committed to that goal?

What was has been the most useful to me?

What have I learned about why I make the choices I do?

Does being self-injurious really help me manage my life?

What do I want in my life bad enough to change my thoughts, feelings or behaviors? What do I need to do to achieve it? How do I demonstrate willingness?

Am I willing to say that maybe I do SOME THINGS RIGHT OR WELL?

Write a positive self-affirmation to encourage yourself!

Slowly breathe and center yourself. Picture yourself accepting this encouragement.

Draw a symbol representing encouragement, calmness and hope.

Exercise 14: What is holding me back?

Shallow men believe in luck. Strong men believe in cause and effect.
Ralph Waldo Emerson
Sometimes life gets in the way of reaching our goals. Sometimes we get in our own way.

What is holding me back in my life?

Where do I want to be in my life?

Obstacles that get in my way of moving towards my goals include:

Goal (what I want)	Obstacles (what gets in my way)	What I can do to overcome

Sometimes things are really tough, and if we want to accomplish something, we have to stay focused even if it is hard to do. How do you do this?

What I can say to myself if I get discouraged:

Write a positive self-affirmation to encourage yourself!

Slowly breathe and center yourself. Picture yourself accepting this encouragement.

Exercise 15: Step by Step Skill Building OR Practice makes Progress

It's not what you have; it's what you do with what you have. Alfred Adler

Identify _one thing_ that you are working on learning how to do differently or better.

Why is this change or growth so hard for you?

What happens inside you that keeps you wanting to go back to doing it the same old way?

How helpful is that for you? What is the cost of repeating the cycle?

 Can you think of something that you learned how to do and involved a lot of practicing? What was that process like for you? What were the pieces of that learning curve? First, second......etc.

Break down your goal into different steps.

Step/Goal	Behavior	Difficulty	What I'll do to manage

Exercise 16: What would you say?

I give myself very good advice, but I very seldom take it. Alice, Alice in Wonderland.

Consider yourself as another person, someone you care about greatly. What problem are you trying to help yourself figure out? What advice would you give about being discouraged, frustrated, angry, hurt, confused or lost? What would you say to you about this problem, if you were a friend?

Dear ....,

What keeps you from allowing yourself to be kind to you when you are struggling?

Am I willing to practice kindness & compassion to myself?   YES or NO?_____

Slowly breathe and center yourself. Picture yourself accepting this encouragement.

Exercise 17: Owning Myself

Identify your BASIC HUMAN RIGHTS – The Bill of Your Rights (list at least 10 rights)

How can you practice these Rights in your life?

Are you willing to live congruently with these Rights? (That means do what you say; say what you mean, live like you believe).

How do you demonstrate respect and dignity to yourself? (That you are worth being treated with respect and dignity.)

Slowly breathe and center yourself. Picture yourself accepting this respect & dignity.

Exercise 18: Protection, Preparation and Anticipation

You could not step into the same rivers; for other waters are ever flowing on to you. Heraclitus

Once I was unaware that I was unable to_____

| And I felt | I thought | I behaved | I believed |

Then I became aware that I was unable to_____

| And I felt | I thought | I behaved | I believed |

Then I became aware that I was able to_____

| And I felt | I thought | I behaved | I believed |

Then I finally became unaware that I was able to _____

| And I felt | I thought | I behaved | I believed |

What have you learned about yourself?

As you begin to grow, think differently about something, it can cause you to be scared. What are helpful ways you can protect yourself when you feel scared or angry?

What are some ways you can be safe when trying something different?

As you change how you do things, sometimes people in your life don't like when you set limits or act differently. What can you anticipate coming as a result of changing the pattern?

What can you do to manage your own reactions to acting differently?

Exercise 19: Alternatives

Recovery Goal:

Identify the ways that you think, feel and react when you feel threatened either externally or internally. These perceptions may get in the way of moving towards your goal. Identify 10-15 ways.

Current Coping Strategies   Identify Healthier Choices

How much do I want to be healthier?
What does "healthier" mean to me? Is it truly healthier – keeping me safe and well?

What am I willing to try the next time I have a chance?

Exercise 20: Recognition and Rewards

Motivation is what gets you started. Habit is what keeps you going. Jim Ryun

Reflect on your efforts towards your goals. How are you doing on this journey?

What are some things you have found yourself doing or thinking about differently?

What is the smallest step and/or change you have made? How do you measure it?? How hard was it for you? What made you be willing to do this? What is something encouraging you could say to yourself about your efforts?

What about some middle-sized changes d/or change you have made? How do you measure it? How hard was it for you? What made you be willing to do this? What is something encouraging you could say to yourself about your efforts?

What is the biggest effort and/or change you have made? How do you measure it? How hard was it for you? What made you be willing to do this? What is something encouraging you could say to yourself about your efforts?

Exercise 21: Shoulds, Wants, Needs and Values

Self-development is a higher duty than self-sacrifice. Elizabeth Cady Stanton

"Should's" hold us prisoners in our own lives if we allow them. "Wants" often are not truly good to us, and serve masters that are not healthy for us. "Needs" are often ignored in service to those unhealthy masters. "Values" are often compromised in our disloyalty to ourselves.

These belief systems govern our choices and behaviors.

Think of a list of "Should's" you operate your life around. List 3-5. Are they helpful?

Think of a list of "Wants" you operate your life around. List 3-5. Are these reasonable?

Think of a list of "Needs" you operate your life around. List 3-5. Are these healthy?

Think of a list of "Values" you operate your life around. List 3-5. Do you base your decisions on them?

How do any of these items help your BASICS? Do they help you be healthy?

What are you willing to do differently to be healthy?

Slowly breathe and center yourself. Picture yourself moving towards living without self-destructive thoughts and behaviors.

Exercise 22: Creating a Motto

If you don't stand for something, you might just fall for anything

What *five – ten words* would *you* like to use to describe you?

What is your life motto?

What does it mean about you?

What five words would you like to be used to describe you (what do you want to become)? What positive values do you practice?

What does this mean about you?

How can you become more like those words?

Slowly breathe and center yourself. Picture yourself becoming who you want to be.

Exercise 23: Human Rights, Personal Beliefs, and ME

The ultimate measure of a man is not where he stands in moments of comfort and convenience, but where he stands at times of challenge and controversy. Martin Luther King, Jr.

We tend to have a pattern of habits to maintain our own sense of status quo. *Sometimes the status quo we work so hard to maintain is not healthy for us.* At one time it may have been helpful to get through a time or circumstance, but it may not be as helpful or healthy to us now.

As we work to become healthier and change old patterns, it may be difficult, *in part because we don't value or respect our own dignity as a person.* We may not act in ways that are respectful to ourselves.

Another aspect of change involves how others react when we change. Sometimes others may not like your behavior as you set limits, say no, or react differently. Often there is a heavy feeling of pressure to keep things the same. Maybe those relationships aren't healthy or good for you.

List at least 10 Human Rights that you believe *all* people should be entitled to be granted.

List Personal Beliefs based on those Human Rights you are willing to work towards keeping and *practicing yourself. What behaviors, thoughts or believes are you willing to try?*

What are some challenges that you may face if you begin to act like you believe you have rights?

Who are you afraid is going to challenge you?
For example, if you believe that people should be treated with respect, maybe one person who may challenge this is *you*, if you believe being self-destructive is acceptable.

How are you going to manage this aspect of your own SECURITY?

Slowly breathe and center yourself. Picture yourself treating yourself with respect & rights.

Exercise 24: Recognizing Unhealthy Patterns & Seeing Accountability

Practice is the best of all instructors. Publilius Syrus

When I_____, I feel _____,

I think _____ ,then I (behavior)

_____

What happens then?_____

When I_____, I feel _____,

I think _____ ,then I (behavior)

_____

What happens then?_____

When I_____, I feel _____,

I think _____ ,then I (behavior)

_____

What happens then?_____ _____

When I_____, I feel _____,

I think _____ ,then I (behavior)

_____

What happens then?_____

When I_____, I feel _____,

I think _____ ,then I (behavior)

_____

Pick one place where you could ACT differently. If you ACT differently, how might the next part of the pattern be different? Then what? How might it end?

Pick one place where you could REACT/FEEL differently (yes, you can choose to feel different!). If you REACT/FEEL differently, how might the next part of the pattern be different? Then what? How might it end?

Pick one place where you could THINK differently. If you THOUGHT differently, how might the next part of the pattern be different? Then what? How might it end?

If you consider yourself a fine gemstone, you'd see there is one major facet and all the other sides of the stone that give it its depth, color and beauty. A flat stone has none of this. You, like a gemstone has lots of different sides contributing to your unique being.

If you consider yourself as a whole being, you lose the fact that you are in fact full of many different qualities, interests, viewpoints, ideas, skills, limits, capacities, knowledge, wisdom, and so on and so on.....

Below use the space as though you are a big jigsaw puzzle. Take the space below and give yourself an outline, and fill it in! Use words, symbols, colors, pictures, whatever you want!

First say to yourself what you would be; and then do what you have to do.

Epictetus

Exercise 26: Allowing Myself to be "in process" of being Whole

My name is....
I stand for...

Three things I believe...

I stand for...

A symbol that represents me is..........................because....................

Draw it

I am becoming............(draw it too)

A motto that represents my beliefs....................................

What are some behaviors that show that I live these ideas? (This is called congruence).

Exercise 27: Holding on, feeding old monsters.....letting go.......

Write yourself a letter about what you want to let go of as part of your growing. Focus on something you need to let go of, old hurts and memories. You don't have to hash out the memories or experiences that may not be helpful, but decide to move them into your past as you move into your future.

Part of moving into your future is recognizing the past experiences may influence your present and future, but don't have to RULE your present and future.

What can you put into a box to be put away, and not let it rule your life anymore.

Think about WHO or WHAT you might need to let go of if you want to be healthy and safe?

You can not change the past, but you can change what it means to you in the present.
You are the author of your present and future.

Exercise 28: Today I Saw an Opportunity

We are shaped by our thoughts. We become what we think. Buddha

Write a letter to yourself about what opportunities you took today to:
1. Try something new
2. To learn something new
3. To see yourself as a healthy person

Write a positive statement about OPPORTUNITIES you can create

Slowly breathe and center yourself. Picture yourself creating opportunities.

What opportunity did you create today?

Exercise 29: Today I tried on something different

Think about a time today when you tried something different than you've done before. What did you do today that was something new? What was it like? Did it end up like you wanted it? Are you willing to try it again?

Give yourself permission to try something new tomorrow. Think about being willing and courageous. What are you going to do?

Give yourself encouragement to do this action.

Slowly breathe and center yourself. Picture yourself giving yourself encouragement and acceptance.

Exercise 30: Today I choose

One can choose to go back toward safety or forward toward growth. Growth must be chosen again and again; fear must be overcome again and again. Abraham Maslow

Today I choose:

To try…………

To do………..

To believe……..

To practice……..

To set limits (how)………….

To challenge…………..

To become……………

To focus on…………

To set limits on…….

I am mindful of…………

Write yourself a positive statement about today.

Slowly breathe and center yourself. Picture yourself accepting this encouragement.

Exercise 31: Faith and Perseverance...and *Willingness*

Faith is believing without necessarily seeing.
Life happens, whether we take responsibility and manage it or not.

What are you willing to believe in? List at least 10 things you are willing to believe in.

How can you practice each of these? Think about your Safety, Security and Physical Well-Being.

A word of encouragement.......
I have the courage to keep managing, making decisions in my own best interest. If I don't make decisions myself, circumstances often make them for me. I may not like the consequences, and have to live with them anyway. I would rather make my choices and live with my own consequences in a way that helps my best interests.

Add your own............

Slowly breathe and center yourself. Picture yourself accepting this encouragement. Allow yourself to experience feeling positive and supported in a healthy way.

Exercise 32: Writing a Good-bye to Self-Destructive Behaviors

Write a letter telling your self-destructive behaviors that you are willing to try other healthier behaviors. Tell your self-destructive behaviors about how they are no longer helpful to you.

Slowly breathe and center yourself. Picture yourself letting go of something you don't need. Give yourself permission to allow your feelings to exist without harming yourself.

Using symbols, pictures, words, and colors, draw letting go of your self-destructive behaviors.

Exercise 33: Dialogue about Feeling

Every feeling has a beginning, middle and an end.
Feelings are data, with intensity, and aren't always accurate. All data needs to be verified.

Name one feeling or experience that is you have had:

What kind of behavior usually happens when you have that feeling? Do you talk to someone, exercise, cry, hurt yourself?

What was going on when that happened? Who was there?

Write a letter to a feeling and tell it how you are going to manage it differently.

Next time, I will slow myself down, using my breathing, pay attention & decide how to respond.

Slowly breathe and center yourself. Picture yourself being mindful about your choices. Accept the consequences of the choices you make. Make choices in your own best interests.

Exercise 34: Tolerating Feelings and Reactions

No one ever died from having feelings. But what you do about them can sink or save you.

Think about how you act when you have a really intense feeling and how you react to it. Briefly write about that experience:

What is it that is hard about you having feelings?

When you have intense or big feelings, what can you focus on to help you cope positively? What words could you use?

Think about feelings in terms of INTENSITY on a continuum. Label them about your feelings:

Feeling	0	1				5				10
	Minimum	Very Low Intensity				About Average Intensity				The Most Intense Experience
JOY (example)	OK	CONTENT			Pleasant	Happy			Joy	Laughing until I cry

It helps to think about feelings as BIG or SMALL instead of "good" or "bad" or all or nothing.

Feelings create our reality. The problem is, they're not always accurate.

The feeling I am experiencing right now, on a scale of 1-10 is a _____ .

Words I would use to describe it are:

Is this a positive, negative or neutral state for my body?

Three words to describe what my body is doing with this feeling (i.e., bouncing my leg, tension, etc).

If it were a color or colors, what color/s would it be?

If it were a noise, what sound would it make?

If it had a shape, what shape would it be?

If it had a smell, what would it smell like?

If it had a size, what would that size be?

If it had a temperature, what would that be?

Where in my body does this feeling usually go to tell me that it is here?

What does it do to my body?

If it had words, what would this feeling be saying?

Who would it be saying those words to?

When am I most likely to be having this feeling?

When I have this feeling, I often:

What else could I do when I have this feeling?

Exercise 36: Containment of Feelings

Peace comes from within. Do not seek it without. Buddha

Sometimes feelings and thoughts become so intense, we feel or think like we can't stand it any more. That is one of the many reasons people sometimes use self-destructive behavior. Self-destructive behaviors might give you a short bit of relief, but the original problem is still there. The problem is still there, and the pattern continues on and on.

One thing that we often don't know is this:
Feelings have a BEGINNING, MIDDLE and an END! The MIDDLE sometimes STINKS!

Another thing we often don't think about is this:
You can choose how you respond or think about something.
The last point about feelings is this:
Feelings and thoughts can't hurt you. What you DO about your thoughts and feelings can.

*SO.........*what is the lesson here?
1. Feelings are temporary. You just have to figure out how to tolerate the middle.
2. You can choose how you respond to or feel about something.
3. The behavior you choose can hurt you.

What do you think about this? Is there something you can choose to do differently here?

Slowly breathe and center yourself. Picture yourself tolerating your feelings.

Using pictures, symbols, words, and colors, draw your idea of containment and show how you can contain your feelings safely.

Exercise 37: Recognizing my tools and resources to interrupt patterns

A good plan today is better than a perfect plan tomorrow. George S. Patton

Tools and resources can be helpful to have an inventory of so that you always know what you have available if you need them to help you:

- Problem solve
- Cope
- Calm yourself
- Manage a tough situation
- Find the way when you are lost
- Make it so you can focus when you are feel overwhelmed

Positive coping skills I can use to help me and I can use instead of unhealthy choices:		
Grounding, breathing		

- Yes, fill out each box (!). When you have self-destructive thoughts you do each one for at least ten minutes, move to the next one, and so on, then start over! The goal is to keep yourself SAFE!!! You are safe unless you make an unhealthy choice.
- This is an opportunity to practice tolerating feelings, and managing through something without being self-destructive.

Exercise 38: Choosing Your Best Interest over "Feelings"

The bravest thing you can do when you are not brave is to profess courage and act accordingly. Corra May Harris

The actions of men are the best interpreters of their thoughts. John Locke

Sometimes how we make decisions based on how we feel, not based on what we need (our best interests). Can you think of some examples of how you might do this? List 5-7.

Can you think about opportunities to ACT in your best interest even when your feelings tell you something different?

Slowly breathe and center yourself. Picture yourself taking the risk of trying something new.

Hope is something I hold onto when my vision is not clear. Mine can be the voice pulling me towards something greater than I am at this moment.

What are your hopes for your future? List 5.

For each, think of *one* set of healthy behaviors that you can do so that you can move towards that future.

Think of 10 ways you can encourage yourself when you might be struggling, afraid or discouraged.

Think of ONE way to be mindful about your choices:

Slowly breathe and center yourself. Picture yourself accepting this encouragement.

Exercise 40: Is Self-Destructive Behavior Really Helpful?

Really give this some thought. *Has your self-destructive behavior really been helpful? Do you like where your life is right now? Do you think there is a connection?*

Write yourself an honest letter about this. Be kind, honest and compassionate with yourself, as you would be if you were talking to a friend:

Are you willing to be different?

Are you willing to try something new?

Slowly breathe and center yourself. Picture yourself creating something new.

The purpose of life is a life of purpose. Robert Byrne

Believe it or not, you have choices about the behaviors you do, even the self-destructive ones. Think of why you have used self-destructive behaviors. List them. In the next column, think of at least two other healthier things you are willing to try.

Why I choose to use self-destructive behaviors	Other healthier things I'm willing to try

Pick one healthier behavior that you will practice for a day. When can you use it?

Slowly breathe and center yourself. Picture yourself calming your fears and having strength.

Exercise 42: What I want Someone to Know about Me

An insincere and evil friend is more to be feared than a wild beast; a wild beast may wound your body, but an evil friend will wound your mind. Buddha

This exercise is thinking about what you can say to someone in your life. You don't have to share it. Sometimes, it may be better not to share it. Remember, you can have your *say*, but you may not get your way. That means you can tell someone to not punish you because of your self-destructive behavior, but they might still do that anyway. This letter is about having your *say*.

Think of someone who you think doesn't really know the "true" you. What do you want them to know about you? What do you need from them? What kind of limits do you need to keep safe?

Slowly breathe and center yourself. Picture yourself accepting yourself.

How honest were you? How honest are you willing to be?

Exercise 43: Friend Want Ad

The minute you settle for less than you deserve, you get even less than you settled for.
Maureen Dowd

If you were to write a want ad for a friend, what qualities would you ask for in that person?
Go back to your list of values, and think about your Safety, Security and Physical Well-Being. How can a friend help you with those?

Wanted: A Friend

In exchange, what could you offer?

Could you be your own friend? Write about it.

Slowly breathe and center yourself. Picture yourself accepting yourself as a friend.

Think of some healthy rules and roles for friendships. Compare your relationships to that list. Who is able to provide elements of healthy relationships, who might not be able to be healthy? Make a list.

Exercise 44: Letter to Someone Who Isn't Good for Me

The minute you settle for less than you deserve, you get even less than you settled for.
Maureen Dowd

Sometimes when we are trying to be healthy, people and relationships in our lives aren't helpful. This can be really sad, make us angry and hurt. Sometimes we fear being alone so much that we stay in relationships that aren't good for us. We even put up with abuse, neglect and unhealthy rules.

Think about someone in your life right now. If you were thinking about what you need from them, what would you ask from them? What do you from the friendship to be healthy? Can they give it to the relationship? What would the relationship need to be healthy?

Do you think they can give it to you? What if they said no, or weren't able to?

Sometimes to create Security and Safety in our world, we need to look at changing how we *relate to relationships*. This is a *mindful* approach to managing ourselves in the context of a relationship with another. This means deciding how we are going to manage ourselves in relationships, how close we let people be to us, how willing we are to let them hurt us or impact our thoughts and feelings. It is about using DATA to help us relate to another.

Something to think about: Some relationships can't give us what we need to be healthy. Sometimes we hold on to relationships because they are comfortable, even though they don't fit us any more. Being alone in a relationship that is unhealthy is far worse and disrespectful to yourself than leaving the relationship to create healthier ones. We can't change someone else, but we can manage how we relate to that relationship.

Can you think of relationships like this? Why or why not? What can you do?

> *Slowly breathe and center yourself. Picture yourself being able to ask for respect and expect it.*

Exercise 45: Life Journey

> One can choose to go back toward safety or forward toward growth. Growth must be chosen again and again; fear must be overcome again and again. Abraham Maslow

One this page, draw your life line, and the lessons you've learned about life. Think about how they have made you the person you are today.

From your life, what piece of wisdom you can teach someone from lessons you've learned?

Exercise 46: My Choices

Action expresses priorities. Mohandas Gandhi

Think of 10 things you are doing differently today than when you started working in recovery.

List them. How has then been helpful to you?

What has been the biggest struggle and why?

Knowing this, how have your choices helped you create Safety, Security & Physical Well-Being?

Slowly breathe and center yourself. Picture yourself being mindful about your Safety, Security & Physical Well-Being.

Be the change that you want to see in the world.
Mohandas Gandhi

What will you miss most if letting go of self-destructive behaviors?

What was the cost of using them? How were they harmful?

How were they helpful? If you looked at the big picture, has your self-destructive behavior been helpful to you?

Write an obituary for your self-destructive behaviors.

Using pictures, words, symbols and colors, draw letting go of your self-destructive behaviors.

Slowly breathe and center yourself. Picture yourself letting go of unhealthy behaviors.

Exercise 48: Self-Respect and Honesty – Taking a Psychological Survivor Position

You can search throughout the entire universe for someone who is more deserving of your love and affection than you are yourself, and that person is not to be found anywhere. You yourself, as much as anybody in the entire universe deserve your love and affection.
Buddha

"Psychological position" is the way we think about something, and it determines how we act towards something. There are basically two positions: Active or Passive. *These are patterns of thinking, behaving and reacting to the world.*
- VICTIM POSITION: passive, avoidant, reactive, driven by feelings, sees the world as random, feels powerless, angry or sad.
- SURVIVOR POSITION: active, direct, proactive, thought/data driven, sees cause and effect that they manage their own reactions to, manages thoughts and feelings by making decisions based on goals and values.

Think about a challenge that you had today, such as wanting to be self-destructive or making a healthier choice. Write about what taking a psychological victim position would look like, and then what a psychological survivor position would look like.

Psychological Victim Position

Psychological Survivor Position

Which do you think is harder, and why?

Which is healthier for you?

Exercise 49: Being Committed to Yourself & Your Future

A small body of determined spirits fired by an unquenchable faith in their mission can alter the course of history. Mohandas Gandhi

In working in this journal, your values and commitment to yourself are directly connected to your goals. Your goal is connected to creating a different tomorrow for yourself than today.

What do you imagine your life will be like in 1-year, if you are truly willing to give up being self-destructive and work on maintaining your Safety, Security and Physical Well-Being?

What needs to be different than today to help you do this?

Slowly breathe and center yourself. Picture yourself creating something new.

It's not what you look at that matters, it's what you see.
Henry David Thoreau

We use pictures, colors and symbols in everyday life. Think of your favorite item, does it have a logo? A logo is a symbol that represents something. Think about what symbols could represent you.

Think of *three* words that you believe strongly represent you. For example, Honesty. Now think of a symbol, color or picture that represents that word.

Write a statement that gives you hope. Let this be your *Mindful Motto*, something you move towards:

Draw a symbol, like a logo, add your Mindful Motto:

Exercise 51: My Own LOGO: My Personal Crest

Try not to become a man of success but a man of value. Albert Einstein

This is your Crest. Your personal crest represents important aspects of you as a whole person. Each part of the Crest represents something different about you. Use words, symbols, colors, pictures

1	What gives you strength	4	What gives you hope
2	What you value in your world	5	What you believe in
3	Symbols that represent you	6	Animal symbol that represents you

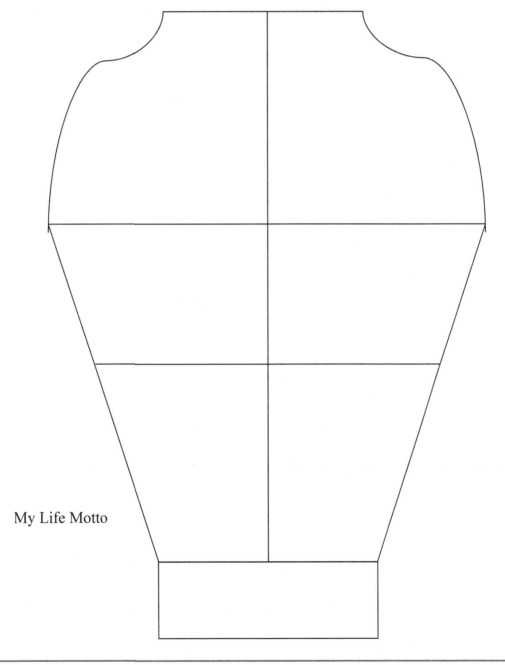

My Life Motto

Exercise 52: My Personal Creed

So long as there is breath in me, that long I will persist. For now I know one of the greatest principles on success; if I persist long enough I will win. Og Mandino

It is important to know what you stand for and what you believe. These are your operating rules and that are your "blueprint" for living. In this exercise, think about these and write your rules:

I believe:

The rules for relationships with me:

What is important to me, and how I say mindful of my goals?

My statement about being in charge of me and my life:

References

Andover, M. S., Pepper, C. M., Ryabchenko, K. A., Orrico, E. G., & Gibb, B. E. (2005). Self-mutilation and symptoms of depression, anxiety, and borderline personality disorder. *Suicide and Life-Threatening Behavior, 35*, 581-591.

Bennewith, O., Stocks, N., Gunnell, D., Peters, T. J., Evans, M. O., & Sharp, D. J. (2002). General practice based intervention to prevent repeat episodes of deliberate self harm. *BMJ: British Medical Journal, 1254*, 324-328.

Brown, M. Z., Comtois, K. A., & Linehan, M. M. (2002). Reasons for suicide attempts and nonsuicidal self-injury in women with borderline personality disorder. *Journal of Abnormal Psychology, 111*, 198-202.

Gratz, K. L. (2001). Measurement of deliberate self-harm: Preliminary data on the Deliberate Self-Harm Inventory. *Journal of Psychopathology and Behavioral Assessment, 23*, 253-263.

Gratz, K. L. (2006). Risk factors for deliberate self-harm among female college students: The role and interaction of childhood maltreatment, emotional inexpressivity, and affect intensity/reactivity. *American Journal of Orthopsychiatry, 76*, 238-250.

Hurry, J. (2000). Deliberate self-harm in children and adolescents. *International Review of Psychiatry, 12*, 31-36.

Isacsson, G., & Rich, C. L. (2001). Management of patients who deliberately harm themselves. *BMJ: British Medical Journal, 322*, 213-215.

Jacobson, C. M. & Gould, M. (2007). The epidemiology and phenomenology of non-suicidal self-injurious behavior among adolescents: a critical review of the literature. *Archives of Suicide Research, 11*, 129-147.

Klonsky, E. D. & Meuhlenkamp, J. J. 2007. Self-injury: a research review for the practitioner. *Journal of Clinical Psychology, 63, 1045-56.*

Levitt, J. L. A self-regulatory approaches to the treatment of eating disorders and self-injury, in Levitt, J. L., Sansone, R. A., & Cohn, L. (Eds.) (2004). *Self-harm behavior and eating disorders: dynamics, assessment, and treatment.* New York, NY: Brunner-Routledge.

Lloyd-Richardson, E. E., Perrine, N., Dierker, L. & Kelly, M. L. (2007). Characteristics and functions of non-suicidal self-injury in a community sample of adolescents. *Psychological Medicine, 37*, 1183-1192.

Nock, M. K. & Cha, C. B. (2009). Psychological models of Nonsuicidal self-injury, Understanding Nonsuicidal self-injury: origins, assessment, and treatment, Nock, M.K., (ed). Washington, D. C.: American Psychological Association

Nock, M. K., Holmberg, E. B., Photos, V. I., & Michel, B. D. (2007). Self-injurious thoughts and behaviors interview: development, reliability, and validity in an adolescent sample. *Psychological Assessment, 19*, 309-317.

Nock, M. K., & Kessler, R. C. (2006). Prevalence of and risk factors for suicide attempts versus suicide gestures: analysis of the National Comorbidity Survey. *Journal of Abnormal Psychology, 115*, 616-623.

Nock, M. K. & Mendes, W. B. (2008). Physiological arousal, distress tolerance, and social problem-solving deficits among adolescent's self-injurers. *Journal of Consulting and Clinical Psychology, 76*, 26-38.

Nock, M. K., & Prinstein, M. J. (2004). A functional approach to the assessment of self-mutilative behavior. *Journal of Consulting and Clinical Psychology, 72,* 885-890.

Nock, M. K., & Prinstein, M. J. (2005). Clinical features and behavioral functions of adolescent self-mutilation. *Journal of Abnormal Psychology, 114,* 140-146.

Ross, S., Heath, N. & Toste, J. R. (2008). Non-suicidal self-injury and eating pathology in high school students. *American Journal of Orthopsychiatry, 1,* 83-92.

Suyemoto, K. L. (1998). The functions of self-mutilation. *Clinical Psychology Review, 18,* 531-554.

Whitlock, J., Eckenrode, J., & Silverman, D. (2006). Self-injurious behaviors in a college population. *Pediatrics, 117,* 1939-1948.